A Stranger In

Zion

ΒΟ∞ĊЯ

A Stranger In

Zion

୫୦ଓଓ

A Christian's Journey through the Heart of Utah Mormonism

Clare Goldsberry

A Stranger in Zion: A Christian's Journey through the Heart of Utah Mormonism
By Clare Goldsberry
Copyright © 2000, 2002 Clare Goldsberry
Published by:
ProWrite Communications
4401 E. Willow Ave.
Phoenix, AZ 85032
Phone: (602) 996-6499

Publisher's Cataloging-in-Publication
(Provided by Quality Books, Inc.)
Goldsberry, Clare, 1947-
A stranger in Zion : a Christian's journey through the heart of Utah Mormonism / Clare Goldsberry. — 1st ed.
  p. cm.
Includes bibliographical references and index.
LCCN: 2001094930
ISBN: 0-9670690-0-9

1. Goldsberry, Clare, 1947- 2. Mormons—Utah—Biography. 3. Church of Jesus Christ of Latter-day Saints. 4. Mormon Church—Utah. I. Title.
BX8695.G65G65 2001   289.3'092
                         QBI01-201234

06 05 04 03 02 5 4 3 2 1

Editor: Gwen Henson
Typesetting: SageBrush Publications, Tempe, Arizona
Cover Design: Karl Reque

Dedication

To my four wonderful children, Keith, Lori, Matthew, and Bryan, whose patience with me as I struggled to find my spiritual path gave me strength and taught me to be patient with them as they seek their own spiritual paths.

This book is a true story based on events of my life during the time I lived in Kaysville, Utah, and shortly after moving to Arizona. However, to protect the privacy of friends and acquaintances, I have changed their names and other identifying references. Only historical figures and family members (Dee Goldsberry and my children, Keith, Lori, Matthew and Bryan) are still identifiable, along with names of General Authorities of the Church of Jesus Christ of Latter-day Saints and other on-the-record sources quoted and used as a result of the research for this book.

ॐ

Contents

Introduction

ഇ⊂ര

Into The Fold

$\mathcal{M}$ormonism, as the religion of those who belong to the Church of Jesus Christ of Latter-day Saints is called, is a purely American religion. Born on the frontier of western upstate New York out of the religious fervor known as the Second Great Awakening, which swept this new nation during the first three decades of the Nineteenth Century, Mormonism has always struggled to exist within the framework of mainstream American Christianity. At the same time, it attempts to remain separate and apart from both Catholicism and Protestantism. It at once desires to be recognized as a part of Christianity, yet more strongly wants to be seen as separate, unique, and the only "true" church of which God approves.

From its beginning, Mormonism has always had its detractors and critics, both from the outside and inside the church. As the church migrated from city to city in what then was then the new frontier of Ohio, then Missouri and on to Illinois, it met with resistance. That resistance was not so much because of beliefs in angels coming to earth with golden plates, or that Joseph Smith saw God and Jesus Christ, or even that it eventually took up the practice of having multiple wives known as polygamy. All of those things were accepted as commonplace in an era when new religions were springing up along the frontier almost weekly in response to the guarantees of religious freedoms upon which this new nation was founded. People tolerated and accepted the excesses and strange practices of many of these new religions almost unilaterally, given that in the early 1800s people changed their religious affiliation nearly as often as they did their underwear.

Religious revival meetings or "camp" meetings, as they were called, facilitated these frequent conversions from one religion to another. People met in large numbers, pitched their tents, and spent days listening to the various preachers from a variety of denominations, each trying to convince listeners that his doctrine was the one to follow. In his book *Religion in America*, Winthrope S. Hudson describes this period of time as one in which heightened religious interests would fan the spark of conversion into a wildfire that would take another twenty years to die down. In fact, that area of upstate New York where Joseph Smith's family resided had experienced so many religious conversions from the various churches it became known as the "burned-over district."[1]

Some historians say it was the Mormons' attitude that often riled peoples' passions against the group. That Mormons believed they were destined to establish God's kingdom on earth—the kingdom of the saints called Zion—on this continent, and specifically in Jackson County, Missouri, put them at odds with many citizens whose land they wanted. When the final blow came, Nauvoo, Illinois, a thriving, bustling city on the banks of the Mississippi River, was as close as the group ever

---

1   *Religion in America*, Winthrope S. Hudson, Charles Scribner's Sons, 1965, pp. 134-141.

came to establishing that kingdom in the East. Mobs of angry men attacked the city and burned the Mormons out, forcing them to withdraw almost completely from the East and retreat to a place where they most assuredly would be left alone to practice their beliefs in peace and establish their kingdom as they believed was their destiny: the largely uninhabited West.

The Mormons started out across the plains in 1847, led by a strong-willed successor to Joseph Smith (who had been murdered while in jail in Carthage, Missouri), named Brigham Young. The group did not really know where it was heading other than west. A few months later, Young announced from a point high above the Great Salt Lake Valley in Emigration Canyon that "this is the place." At Young's direction, the group settled in a harsh environment where the only water visible was unfit to drink because of its high salt content. However, the Mormons had faith in and followed their leader unquestioningly, as they had been taught to do. They overcame problems such as the lack of fresh water by building canals to channel mountain streams. When crickets nearly destroyed the first year's crops, they were saved thanks to multitudes of sea gulls that came from nowhere and ate the crickets—one of many Mormon "miracles." Young commissioned Porter Rockwell and his vigilante "avenging angels" to keep the Valley free of those who could ever again make life for the Mormons impossible. They handled threats from the outside world in the form of other settlers, many of whom met their death at the hands of the vigilantes. Thus was established this country's first theocracy. The Mormon people built their kingdom of Zion, known to the secular world as Salt Lake City, and set about to make the "desert blossom as a rose" as ordained in their scripture, the Book of Mormon.

Brigham Young originally intended to make the Utah territory an independent nation, a true theocracy self-sufficient from the rest of the country. Plans called for the Utah territory to include Utah, most of Nevada, Arizona, and a strip into Southern California that would include present-day Santa Barbara to give the "nation" its own seaport. However, the federal government did not look kindly on that plan, and so the people sought to make Utah a state instead.

Although the church had to relinquish the "law" of polygamy in order to obtain statehood, the Manifesto of 1893 was a change in doctrine not welcomed by some Mormons, particularly those with several wives and many children. Rather than deny polygamy and put out their wives and children to exist without means of support, these men moved with their large families to territories in Arizona, Northern Mexico, and even Canada, where polygamy is still practiced today in many of those communities established at the turn of the century to accommodate the beliefs of the Mormon "fundamentalists" as they came to be called.

Today, Utah continues to be the closest thing to a theocracy that exists among the fifty United States of America. Only in recent years have non-Mormons, who are becoming more populous in the state, gained a toehold in government. In a place where there are more Mormons than anything else, particularly in rural areas, and because Mormons typically vote for Mormons, those elected to government offices have been primarily Mormon. Many of the state's laws continue to reflect Mormon doctrine, however in recent years many of the laws have changed to give the state a more "secular" appearance and opening it up even further to the world. With the Winter Olympics slated for 2002, the world will pour into Utah and into the Salt Lake Valley. Certainly the influences that Brigham Young sought to escape 150 years ago will confront Utah Mormonism in new and challenging ways.

The church (When you say "The Church" in Utah, it is assumed that it is the Mormon Church since that is the only one recognized officially.) continues to have a major influence on decisions to change the laws to be more accommodating to events such as the Winter Olympics, placing its blessings on those changes in order to win the popular support of the people. In Utah, perhaps more than in any other state, the Mormon people follow the voice of their church leaders. The leaders have powerful influence over the vote of the people, despite the claim that the church does not dictate how its members should vote or that it uses its pulpits to support a particular candidate.

In spite of attempts by the church to keep itself a separate and unique religion, in recent years it has shown a desire to be accepted as a "Christian" religion. To improve its public image, Mormonism has attempted to remove the stigma of "cult" with which its critics have painted it for more than a century. That is where many of its problems lie. Mormons and non-Mormons alike challenge certain doctrines of Mormonism, and the church has proved that doctrinal change comes slowly, if at all.

One example of change that drew mixed reaction from people both inside and outside the fold came when the church was forced to acknowledge and accept people of color. Suddenly—literally overnight—the church changed its long-standing doctrine banning African-American men from ever holding its priesthood offices. Then came changes in the text of the Book of Mormon, which previously said that Native Americans—if they became Mormon and followed Mormon ways long enough—would become a "white and delightsome" people, proof of God's acceptance of them. Now, says the new Book of Mormon text, they will become a "pure and delightsome" people. Pressure from women, starting in the 1970s with the furor over the Equal Rights Amendment to gain the priesthood and obtain equal status with Mormon men, has resulted in the excommunication of many women and even some men who dared to speak out for this change.

In its attempts to be unique and separate, the church has been in a state of denial about problems that plague many of its members, problems not unlike those from which people everywhere suffer. That the church continues to paint a portrait of itself as the epitome of Christian living, of happy family and social life, flies in the face of the many dichotomies woven into Utah's socio-religious fabric. The social ills that afflict every community also are present in Utah Mormon communities. Yet church leaders continue to attempt to sweep such ills under the rug in order to attain their goal: to make everyone on the face of the earth Mormon and eventually lead the United States of America into a theocracy by saving the Constitution, which they believe someday will become so threatened as to "hang by a thread."

In spite of these attempts to hide its problematic history and unique theology from the outside world, the world cannot help but notice the strange and often baffling occurrences that take place in Utah. There was the case of John Singer, a polygamist and a man who believed in "live and let live" as he taught his children at home. A separatist who wanted nothing to do with the outside world, he was gunned down by law enforcement agents over the fact that he refused to send his children to public school. Then there was the retaliation bombing of a Mormon Church in Singer's community, a crime for which the Singer family paid dearly. There was the case of Mark Hoffmann, a good Mormon with affiliations in the highest places within the church hierarchy. He forged church "historical" documents, then sold them to church leaders who paid a high price to keep the documents, which contained controversial material, from being revealed to the general population of the church. Hoffmann, about whom the world read in the book *The Mormon Murders* by Steven Naifeh and Gregory White Smith, is now serving time in the Utah State Penitentiary for the murders of one of his business partners and the wife of another of his associates, crimes resulting from his attempts to cover-up the forgeries.

The LeBaron clan, an infamous Mormon fundamentalist, polygamous family has run amok in the West for decades killing off each other and members of rival sects. Part of a group of settlers to Northern Mexico during the exodus of polygamous families from Utah at the turn of the Nineteenth Century, LeBaron's group is an enigma to the rest of the modern world for whom religious-based killings in the United States seems unthinkable. Another book, *The Four O'Clock Murders*, details this group's escapades.

Many in this country were shocked to read about, (and later view a made-for-television movie), Richard Worthington of Sandy, Utah, who took a hospital maternity ward hostage, killing a nurse in the process, in an attempt to seek out and kill the doctor who performed a sterilization procedure on his wife.

All these things seem strange and an anathema to those in this country in the Twentieth Century who do not understand how the theology, sociology, and psychology of Mormonism intertwine to create such oddities. That a religion that portrays itself to the world as so good, so peaceful, so righteous and accepted by God as the only true church on earth, can at the same time breed so much bloodshed and horror, seems ironic.

Mormons continue to be as much a curiosity today as they were in the 1800s. Perhaps they are even more difficult for people to understand in today's society. The church continues to grab news headlines, most recently for the ouster of numerous members determined to be dissidents due to their speaking out on issues of church doctrine, calling into question certain doctrines and questioning church leaders, something that is strictly forbidden. This latest purge of some of the church's brightest and best writers, intellectuals, and teachers resulted in more people taking notice of the strange dichotomies that exist within the framework of Mormon theology and in particular within Mormonism's heart, Utah.

Unless one has actually experienced Mormonism from the inside and in Utah, one cannot possibly understand the sociology and psychology of those who adhere to its tenets of faith. This book is an attempt, in some small way, to look at one town, a microcosm of Utah Mormon society, and help people who are curious about Mormonism's ways to understand a group that has become an anomaly to mainstream American religion, even as it has its roots there. It is an attempt to answer some of the many questions I am asked when people find out I used to be a Mormon. Even people who are generally uninterested in religion have a curiosity about the Mormons: who they are, what they practice, and why they are so successful at making converts to a religion comprised of such a nontraditional doctrine.

This was not an easy book to write. My family is now Mormon, and I have many good friends who are Mormon—people whom I love and respect, who have called into question my motives for writing this book. Mormons are unforgiving of anyone who writes less than favorably about them and their religion. Although I am no longer a Mormon, I face further ostracism from my friends and family in the church for writing this book. However, to satisfy others' curiosity, to answer their questions, and perhaps to come to a better understanding myself of what happened to me and why it made such a profound impact on my life, my journey through Mormonism must be told. What follows is the story of my life as a stranger in Zion.

1

⬥⬥⬥

Temple Marriage:
Sacred Secrets

It was supposed to be the most glorious, spiritual day of my Mormon life. Temple marriage is something to which all faithful Mormons aspire with great eagerness and anticipation—the day in which man and woman are "sealed" together for "time and all eternity" to become a family unit forever. To become privy to the "sacred" ceremonies within the temple and learn the secret rites crucial to salvation and entrance into the highest degree of Mormon heaven—the Celestial Kingdom—would mean that I, at last, would be a full-fledged member of the Church of Jesus Christ of Latter-day Saints. I was filled with nervous excitement and eager anticipation to finally obtain the right to enter the temple with all the implications that entrance held. Yet as I began my participation in these rituals within the hallowed walls of the temple in Ogden, Utah, I discovered that I was asked to do and say things that seemed strangely uncomfortable to me—things that caused a chill of fear to run through my body like ice water.

As I pledged the first of three "sacred" blood oaths, which were a vital part of the ceremony, the words of the Mormon bishop who had married my husband, Dee, and me in a civil ceremony two years earlier came back to haunt me. "Do you know what you're getting into by marrying a Mormon?" he asked. At the time I had not realized the full implications of his question or even why it was important for me. Even now, seated in the "theater" with seventy or so other good Mormons who seemed to be thoroughly comfortable and involved with the proceedings, I was not certain what I had gotten myself into by marrying a Mormon. I thought back to that day when I had received my first introduction to Mormon officialdom known as the Bishopric.

Seated in front of the bishop, I tried to act nonchalant as he questioned Dee, the man I wanted to marry, and me about our goals, our hopes, our dreams, and ambitions for the future. I could foresee a future no farther away than marrying this man I had known about four months. He was a wonderful lover and a lot of fun to be with. For young people, such as we were then, criteria like these can seem like the only measurement for spousal material that really matters. The bishop told us we could not have a real wedding in the sanctuary of the church, because the only "real" marriage in the eyes of the Mormon Church was one performed "for time and all eternity" in one of the few Mormon temples scattered throughout the world. To "qualify" for that, one had to be a member of the Mormon Church in good standing for at least one year.[2] That left both of us out. However, the Bishop would perform the ceremony in the Relief Society room, a large, beautifully decorated meeting room named

---

2   To be in good standing, Mormons must be attending church regularly, paying ten percent of their gross income to the church, and participating actively in the life of the ward.

for the church's women's organization, and in which their weekly meetings were held.

What was I getting into? Doubts began to filter into my mind, littering my thoughts as I made promises—blood oaths, actually—to have my life taken if I ever revealed any of the sacred—and very secret—teachings I learned that day in the temple. Saying the words and making the accompanying "signs" that were so alien to anything I'd ever known in my Christian Protestant upbringing, gave me a queasy feeling in the pit of my stomach. As I looked around at all the faithful Mormons whose lives revolve around the church, no one else seemed particularly alarmed at what was said or done, so I tried to take some comfort in that.

I looked across the aisle at my husband, Dee, standing in the required white temple clothing, his dark, wavy hair curling out from underneath the strange-looking hat he and the other men wore. I would never know if this ceremony was something he really wanted or if it was something he did because I had become so entrenched in the religion of his family. We never really spoke about our deep feelings when it came to spiritual matters. I was then and have always been a seeker. Dee had always been certain of the Mormon Church's claim to be the only "true" church on earth. I questioned everything; he questioned nothing. Achieving unity in our thinking did not matter at that point in our lives, but later those differences would haunt us.

As we learned the signs and "tokens" of the two branches of the Mormon priesthood, the Melchizedek and Aaronic, we pledged never to reveal these under penalty of death. As we went through each ritual, I felt a strange sense of panic overcoming my being. My heart was pounding in my ears. I strained to listen to the leader in the front of the room who directed us through the steps. Under my breath, I promised God that if he got me out of this place alive I would never return.

But I would return many more times in my quest to become what at that time I believed I wanted more than anything in the world: to be a good Mormon so that I could be with my husband and children for all eternity. It is a promise to all those who accept the teachings of the Mormon faith and live the laws laid out for them in this life. Although temple marriage is the goal of all faithful Mormons, for various reasons, not all attain it. Going to the temple meant, for me, the culmination of my initiation into Mormonism and the completion of my acceptance into the church. I would be allowed to wear the sacred temple "garments," special underwear, the outline of which I saw every day beneath the clothing of my friends. I had envied them during the time required by the church before my being allowed to go to the temple. Now I would be like them. I would at last be a Mormon of the highest degree—or at least as high as women can expect to attain in Mormonism—counted among the Mormon elite, a part of the exclusive percentage of members that achieves temple marriage. My curiosity about religion in general, and in particular about Mormonism since my marriage to a Mormon, had taken my life along a path that I believed I wanted. Yet participating in this ceremony was causing me to feel strangely uncomfortable. Doubts about what I had done by joining the Mormon Church began to creep over me like a large, dark cloud passing between the sun and earth leaving me to stand in its shadow. I felt a strange chill. I shivered.

To enter the temple requires a recommend, a slip of paper signed by the stake[3] president after a lengthy interview with each person. To Mormons, the possession of a temple recommend is as important in their lives as a driver's license or a social security

---

3   A stake is made up of approximately twelve to thirteen wards, a ward being the individual congregation. A stake president, his two counselors, and other assistants who oversee the wards under their jurisdiction head each stake.

card. Punishment for Mormons who stray from the faith often involves confiscating their temple recommend, as a judge might revoke one's driver's license for a DUI. A recommend must be renewed before its expiration date each year by going through the same interview process as one did initially.

I thought it odd that Dee and I were interviewed separately, almost like a police interrogation of two cohorts in crime to make sure our stories corroborated. But, I was not in a questioning mood at that time. I answered the questions I was asked and accepted the process—as I had accepted the other processes up to this point—as necessary to ensure my eternal happiness in the Celestial Kingdom.

The questions were innocuous enough: Do you obey the Word of Wisdom (the rules against smoking and drinking of alcohol, tea, or coffee)? Do you attend church regularly and participate in the life of the church? Are you morally clean? Do you pay a full tithe? It did not occur to me until nearly nine years later, when I was finally making my way out of the maze of Mormonism, how ridiculous the questions were.

According to Mormon dictates, no one can enter the highest degree of heaven and be with his family for eternity unless he goes to the temple, receives his "endowments," makes all the proper pledges and promises, and learn all the signs and symbols. Therefore, one can be denied this privilege—and never see one's family again—simply because one drinks a cup of coffee in the morning. Several years later, discovering that I was spiritually bankrupt, I stopped dead in my tracks one day to ponder the terrible implications of this process that denied people access to their families for eternity. Not that this belief is true, but people believe it is true. For them, it becomes their reality—often resulting in spiritually damaging consequences. Reaching that conclusion many years later, I broke down in tears, utterly ashamed that I had ever embraced such a terrible, exclusive doctrine. It had the potential to ruin lives—and in fact did ruin many lives—and cause such earthly grief. What had once seemed wonderful suddenly became ludicrous.

At that time, however, I obeyed the rules of the church. My husband and I passed the first phase of our interview with the bishop of our ward with flying colors. Then we went for a second interview with the stake president. It was basically a repeat of the first interview. We answered the same questions, while this man—this priesthood holder who, like all priesthood holders, had the authority to act for God on earth—judged whether we were worthy to go to the most holy of holy houses of the Lord God of Mormonism. In the end, (much to my relief) we were found worthy and the stake president signed the slips of paper that would grant us admittance to the temple in Ogden, Utah, where we would become a family forever. It was, I thought then, one of the happiest days of my life.

On the day of our temple marriage, we were escorted to the temple by two carloads of friends from the ward who went with us to show us the ropes, so to speak. I felt strangely frightened. My heart was pounding as we approached the temple with its quietly elegant—and crossless—spire pointing heavenward. The lack of Christian symbolism in the Mormon Church was something else that bothered me throughout those years. I knew that Mormons felt the cross represented the death of Christ, and they preferred to celebrate his resurrection. Still, it was one more small thing that Mormons used to separate themselves from the Christian world, and it made me, as a Christian, uncomfortable. As we walked through the glass doors I thought my heart would burst with joy (or maybe it was fear—my emotions seemed confused, and I felt unsteady) at finally being able to walk on such holy ground.

An older woman dressed in a floor-length white dress took our daughter in her arms to a nursery. She and her brother, my seven-year-old son, Keith, by my short-lived marriage to my high school sweetheart, would wait for us to finish the endowments before being reunited with us in the "sealing" room.[4] An elderly gentleman, (almost all the temple workers are retired people with the time to dedicate to working every weekday in the temple) also clad in a completely white suit, stood behind a desk at the entrance to check the validity of our recommends, like being carded at a nightclub. We were told to enter and get a nametag.

The others in our group were given the names of deceased people, for whom they would receive the endowments by proxy. This was to enable those who had not had a chance in this life to hear and accept the "true" gospel of Mormonism the opportunity to get to the highest degree of heaven, even though they were already in a spirit world somewhere. The names of the deceased people came from genealogy records sent in by the person's family. Thousands of names are submitted daily from records around the world by people diligently performing their genealogy work in order to "save" their dead ancestors. Even the founding fathers of the United States have had their temple work done, something which I am certain has Thomas Jefferson turning over in his grave.

It all seemed so tidy and neat and wonderful at the time—the prospect that everybody can be one big happy, heavenly family in the next life. It wasn't until later that I tried figuring out just how this was supposed to work. If husbands and wives and their children were sealed together, and their children grow up to be sealed to their wives and children, and each man is to go off into his own sphere in the universe to create spirit children for other worlds, then how is it that everyone can stay together?

---

4   The sealing room is a small, high-ceilinged room lined with mirrors, which made it look as if it went on forever—like eternity, where the actual ceremony is performed that "seals" a family together forever.

Would I stay with my husband or my father? Or would we get trans-celestial visitation rights? Later, as I studied, questioned, and looked even deeper into the theology, it all became even more confusing. There were really no clear-cut answers. No wonder many Mormons choose not to think about things too deeply. Many times I was told that I would just have to take things on faith and that God would work out the details. I came to believe, however, that God was not all that concerned about the details of Mormonism.

Next, we were escorted to an area where we rented our temple clothes. Many people who attend the temple regularly own their temple clothes, because it is cheaper in the long run. But being new, Dee and I had to rent ours. The men and women then went to separate locker rooms to change clothes. Because I was a "new" bride, so to speak, I was led, along with a good friend to help me, to a beautifully decorated room to get dressed. The temple gown I rented was especially frilly, designed to look like a real wedding dress and reserved for first-time temple brides who, like myself, had been married civilly. New brides who are being married for the first time both civilly and in the church usually wear their own gowns. I undressed down to my bare skin. An elderly woman temple worker gave me what appeared to be a sheet with a hole cut in the middle for my head, much like a ghost costume I would make for my son to wear Halloween trick-or-treating.

I was taken to the washing and anointing room where there were several cubicles with curtains. Each cubicle contained a stool that sat on a pedestal about two steps above the floor. There I sat, draped in my sheet, while another elderly woman approached me with a bottle of "consecrated" olive oil (oil blessed by members of the male priesthood and used in special anointing ceremonies like this and to heal the sick). She anointed me, repeating a blessing for each body part. Her oil-covered fingertips brushed lightly across the various parts of my body from the top of my head to my feet, including my shoulders, arms, breasts, and lower stomach (that I might be fruitful and bear many children), loins, thighs, legs, and feet. I felt slightly uncomfortable with this ceremony especially with being touched on my bare skin by a stranger. But I looked at her, this woman who was probably a wife, mother, grandmother, and, most likely, a lifelong member in good standing in the church, and decided that it was all for a holy purpose.

Lastly, this sister whispered to me my "new name," a name that only my husband would know. He would use it to call me forth in the resurrection to live with him for eternity. Women cannot be resurrected on their own, but their husbands must call them forth at the appropriate time. I often heard my friends' husbands joke with them that if they didn't behave and mind them, they would not call them forth to be resurrected and they would have to stay in the ground forever. The men thought this was funny, but I failed to see any humor in this warped sense of their power over their wives.

The sister helped me climb into the white nylon, one-piece underwear, known as temple garments, which would become my second skin for the rest of my life. The top had a wide neckline that scooped down in the back so I could step into the garment. It had cap sleeves to cover the top of my shoulders and ensure that I would never again wear anything sleeveless. A crotch slit from the back of the waist to the navel in the front enabled me to comfortably go to the bathroom without disrobing. The legs came down to just above my knees, which meant that, from now on, miniskirts and shorts in the summer were out of the question. Mormons are always encouraged to dress conservatively, but young girls who have not yet married in the temple wear typically fashionable clothes including short skirts and shorts. For someone quite comfortable with her sexuality, who

had a good body and did not mind—at age twenty-five—showing it, this was quite a comedown. My days of being sexy, I knew,
were definitely over.[5]

I returned to the beautiful dressing room where I put my
white bra and white panties (white is required for every piece of
clothing) over my temple garment, slipped on my white panty-
hose (also required), and was helped into my "wedding" dress.
As I stood before one of the many ornate mirrors that covered
the walls above the dressing tables, I hardly recognized myself. I
had never worn white for a wedding before. My first marriage
was foisted upon me by parents who believed the only thing for
a pregnant teenager to do was get married. That dress had been
an ugly pink thing, just the color for letting the world know that
I was a tainted bride. For my second marriage—to Dee—the
dress had not been much better. A friend made me a dress from
pale blue satin completely covered in white lace with slender,
lace arms. It definitely outdid the first dress, and the marriage
was something I had wanted, which made the wedding a much
better experience all the way around. But, I had always wanted
to wear a white wedding dress, because deep in my heart I believed I deserved a white dress. Mormonism had given me that
chance. After all, the bishop and the stake president both said I
was "worthy."

Now here I was, standing in a long, white wedding dress,
complete with veil, about to participate in a marriage ceremony
known only to the most faithful Mormon followers, to commit
my life to the church and to Dee for time and all eternity, which
had more far-reaching implications than the ordinary " 'til death
do us part" routine.

---

5   Garments now come in two-piece styles to allow members to wear one
     piece, say the top, when playing tennis in shorts, or just the bottoms should
     men have the need to go shirtless while working outdoors in hot weather.

A white, cloth carrying case held the rest of the garb needed for the mysterious ceremony: a bright green apron sewn in the shape of fig leaves (handmade for me by an elderly friend in the ward whom I grew to love dearly) and a white, pleated, drape-like robe with satin ribbon ties.

My friend—who was dressed completely in white also but in a dress of more simple design—and I were taken to a waiting room that resembled a chapel with rows of pews where our group would wait for an endowment room to become available. I sat down by Dee, who was also dressed in white from head to toe, complete with a bouffant-style hat that flopped over to one side, something like a French impressionist artist would wear while painting voluptuous nude women sprawled on velvet "fainting" couches. I smiled to myself at the image. The hat was tied by a wide, grosgrain ribbon to a loop on his shirt's shoulder to assure that if the hat fell, it wouldn't hit the floor (a no-no). He also carried a white bag containing his fig-leaf apron and pleated robe.

My anticipation heightened as we sat there listening to soft, background organ music. I gripped his hand, my nervousness showing. I really loved this man who had shown me this marvel-ous religion, and now we were about to be assured that we would spend eternity together. Soon a temple worker came into the room and announced in a quietly reverent tone that a room was available for us. We stood and followed him. The entire en-dowment ceremony, at that time, took about ninety minutes since the church had put it on video tape sometime in the late 1960s. Before the use of videotape, temple workers acted out the endowment ceremony and it had taken much longer, I was told.

There were several endowment rooms where ceremonies took place from early morning until late evening every day ex-cept Sunday. We entered the high-ceilinged room through tall, ornate doors. The room was not large, about the size of a small theater with a center aisle and rows of perhaps one hundred theater-like seats on either side. I was led to the first seat on the aisle of the front row of the left-hand side of the room, and Dee was led to the same seat on the right. Others filed in and seated themselves—men on the right side and women on the left.

A large, stage area at the front was hung with beautiful drapes. Since I had no idea what to expect, I just settled in for the ride. The lights dimmed, and the curtains opened, just like a theater. The two temple workers, one female and one male, sat on their respective sides of the room at the front facing us. Their job, as I learned, was to help Dee and I through the intricacies of the ceremony. As the videotape started, the deep, booming voice of the narrator started speaking of the creation of the heavens and earth, as found in the first chapter of Genesis. On the screen were beautiful, National Geographic-like shots of red-hot lava pouring down from a volcano. The scenes changed as the narrator continued to read from Genesis. "Well, so far, so good," I thought, enjoying the beautiful scenery as God separated the darkness from the light and the land from the sea and created all the creatures that ever walked on the face of the earth.

Then we came to the creation of man. In the Bible, there are two accounts of the creation of humans. The first account, found in Genesis 1:26-28, tells of God making Man (using the Hebrew word meaning Mankind) both "male and female," in His image at one time and together. Mormons choose the second account, found in Genesis 2:8-23, in which Eve is formed from Adam's rib, as the true version. Adam, in the temple movie, is a very good-looking young man, and Eve is, of course, beautiful with long, blond hair and a great body (stereotypical of young Mormon women)—what could be seen of it. Because they are both naked at first they are only shown from the shoulders up. In the tape, Eve is out in the Garden of Eden one day when along comes an extremely handsome, (even better look-ing than Adam) dark-haired man with a goatee and mustache, who shows Eve an apple from the tree of knowledge of good and evil. At first Eve resists, because "Heavenly Father" has for-bidden them to eat of that tree. But, Eve succumbs to tempta-tion and takes a bite, then takes the apple to Adam. Because Eve has taken a bite and is now subject to punishment for her dis-obedience, Adam is compelled to take a bite also so that they can remain together as God intended. They see their nakedness and proceed to make for themselves aprons of fig leaves.

The movie stopped, and we were told by the narrator to rise, take our green satin aprons designed to look like sewn-together fig leaves, from the little pouch we carried and tie them around our waists like Adam and Eve did, the aprons symbolizing the fig leaves. We all rose, did as we were instructed, then sat back down. The movie continued.

Adam and Eve are cast out of the beautiful garden and into a dry, desolate world where they will have to work hard to eat and Eve will suffer pain in childbearing. (So much for the benefits of knowledge!) God gives them clothes of animal skins to drape around their bodies. Once again, the movie stopped and we stood, took out our pleated robes, draped them over our left shoulders and tied the front to the back at the waist with the rib-bon. In addition to my temple garments, regular underwear, slip, dress, and apron, I was wearing a long, shear, nylon, pleated "robe" to symbolize Adam and Eve being given clothing to wear before to being cast out of the garden. The men also draped their robes across their bodies. We were all beginning to look a bit bulky.

I was a bit amazed by the ceremony, but not put off by any-thing I had seen or heard so far. However, I was still nervous, and I was disturbed by the theology. Satan convinced Eve that the only reason God did not want Adam and Eve to eat the apple was to keep them from becoming like God. Thus, the desire to be like God is at the heart of Eve's disobedience. Yet, it is every Mormon male's goal to become not just "like" God but actually to become a god. I was already beginning to be confused.

Eventually, I would learn that Mormon theology does not consider what Eve did to be a "sin," because it unlocked the door of godhood for men, who could now become as God. In fact, Joseph Fielding Smith, one of the presidents of the Mormon Church, wrote, "The fall of man came as a blessing in disguise . . . I never speak of the part Eve took in this fall as a sin, nor do I accuse Adam of sin . . . We can hardly look upon anything resulting in such benefits as being a sin." (Doctrines of Salvation, Vol. 1, 1960 ed., pp. 113-115) We sat down, and the movie continued. As Adam and Eve walk along trying to figure out what to do next, the man portraying Satan approaches them and asks them what they are doing wandering around in the world. They say something to the effect that they are trying to find their way back to Heavenly Father.

"I have someone who can help you," Satan says, smiling broadly. At this point, Satan introduces Adam and Eve to a man dressed as a Protestant clergyman with white clerical collar and black coat.

"Here, this man can help you find the path back to Heavenly Father," says Satan.

The Protestant minister then tries to teach Adam and Eve from the Bible. Suddenly, three men dressed in Middle Eastern garb from Biblical times interrupt him. They introduce themselves as Peter, James, and John, and say they will help Adam and Eve discover the path back to Heavenly Father because they have the "truth" about how to find the way.

Satan and his cohort, the Protestant preacher, hang their heads and walk away. I sat there stunned by what I had just seen. My heart was pounding. Suddenly a sense of dread and foreboding came over me. Real fear invaded my whole being. I wanted to jump up and run out of the room. But I couldn't. I was trapped. I was deeply offended by the portrayal of the Protestant minister as a servant of the devil. In all my years of Christian upbringing, I had loved the ministers who served so faithfully and tirelessly in our congregation at Bullittsville Christian Church. They nurtured my faith in God, taught me the Christian way and loved me and supported me during my years of faith development. Those men had been my Christian mentors and helped develop my tremendous interest in religious studies. They were responsible for my deep and abiding love for the scriptures and for God.

My whole body seemed to emanate a white-hot heat. The massive amount of clothing seemed to weigh me down into my seat, refusing to let me up even if I'd had the courage to leave. I thought I was going to be sick. Had I been fooled? I thought the Mormons were respectful of other religions from which they drew many of their converts. I thought they loved everyone. How could it be that they would pass judgement on other Christians, to make them appear to be messengers of Satan?

Silently, fervently I prayed to God to help me understand. Surely there was a reason the Mormons had included this offending scene with Satan and the minister. "Please, God, let me know the truth; let me know why this is."

I began to doubt all that I'd been taught in childhood in Sunday School and church. A wave of confusion swept over me once again. In spite of my strong testimony to the truthfulness of the Mormon Church I suddenly was not sure what was true. I would spend much of my Mormon life in confusion as I delved deeper into Mormon history and theology. Later I learned that Mormons have a wry joke that if a person can go through the temple and come out with his testimony of the church intact, he is probably a member for life.

Unbelievably, the worst part of the ceremony was yet to come. We were next given secret signs and passwords, called "tokens," of both the Aaronic and Melchizedek priesthood, which Mormons believe have been restored from Old Testament times to Joseph Smith. The priesthood is the heart and soul of the church and all Mormon males are ordained into this patriarchal brotherhood at age twelve.

I was becoming appalled and repulsed by what was taking place. After we were given each sign or token, we were also told of an accompanying "penalty" for ever revealing that sign. To seal all that we'd been told we took blood oaths, that rather than reveal anything we had learned in the temple that day, we each would "suffer my life to be taken." Then we made the appropriate sign of how that would take place. The slitting of the throat was symbolized by drawing the thumb of the right hand across the throat from ear to ear; the cutting out of our hearts was symbolized by drawing the thumb of the right hand across one's chest; lastly, disemboweling was symbolized by drawing the thumb of the right hand across the width of one's waist from side to side.

Visions of Satanic cults flashed through my mind. I began fervently praying in my mind again, "Please God, just get me out of here alive, and I'll never come back. Please! Please!" The experience was nothing like anything I had ever known before in my life.

I was not familiar at that time with the Masonic ceremony, but later learned through a male friend who was an inactive Mason of high degree, that the Mormon ceremony is virtually identical to the Masonic ceremony. In fact, we compared the so-called secret "handshake," which in Mormonism is called the Sure Sign of the Nail, wherein little fingers are interlocked and the middle finger of each person's hand is pressed into the center of the wrist of the other person's hand. After giving each other the secret handshake, which we each had learned from two separate ceremonies, I laughed and said, "Well, you know what this means don't you? Either you're a Mormon or I'm a Mason!" Although I thought the remark amusing, deep down inside, I felt that such deception foisted upon several million members of the Mormon Church by their leaders was no laughing matter. Although Mormons frown on the Masonic brotherhood to the extent that Mormons are not permitted to join the Masons, Joseph Smith embraced the organization during the church's time in the city of Nauvoo, Illinois, and himself became a 32nd Degree Mason. Shortly afterward, he introduced the temple ceremony, which was originally for men only, as a part of Mormon priesthood initiation rites. Later, when he instituted polygamy, women were included in the endowment ceremony, and a marriage ceremony was added.

In the next phase of the endowment ceremony, oaths of obedience were taken. Men took an oath to be obedient to God, and women took an oath to be obedient to their husbands as long as they are obedient to God. As we neared the conclusion of the ceremony, a "prayer circle" was formed in which Dee and I were asked to participate with the two temple workers and several others. We stood in a circle at the front of the room and prayed, concluding with the second token of the Melchizedek priesthood, raising both hands above our heads and chanting, as we lowered our hands, "Pay Lay Ale, Pay Lay Ale, Pay Lay Ale."

The movie screen ascended, and the curtains behind it parted to reveal another wall of white curtains. Here we would simulate entering heaven and receive the third token of the Melchizedek priesthood. Several temple workers stood along the back side of the curtain wall, while one at a time, row by row we approached the curtain, called the "veil." In usual endowment ceremonies, a male temple worker stands behind the "veil" to portray God, but for those receiving their endowments for the first time, the husband stands behind the "veil" acting in his role as God. Dee was my "god." A female temple worker helped me with the Five Points of Fellowship while a male temple worker helped Dee on the other side of the curtain. "Inside of right foot by the side of right foot, knee to knee, breast to breast, hand to back, and mouth to ear," resulted in a position that looked similar to two people about to waltz. The contact was made through slits in the curtain at the appropriate places, while the curtain remained between us. Dee asked me through the veil to repeat all the signs, tokens, and symbols, which I obediently did. He then asked for my secret name. "Ruth," I replied. Then he gave me the final token, the secret passwords that would guarantee my entrance into heaven with him: "Health in the navel, marrow in the bones, strength in the loins and in the sinews. Power in the priesthood be upon me and upon my posterity for generations of time and throughout all eternity." He then took my hand, parted the "veil," and pulled me through. I was now in the highest degree of heaven.

As we entered the beautiful Celestial Room, with its high, gilded ceiling, crystal chandeliers and plush, ornate furniture, I released a sigh of relief. I had made it. The sealing ceremony was relatively simple after that. We were led to a small, mirrored room where we knelt on opposite sides of an altar. Our children, my son whom Dee had adopted a year earlier and our eighteen-month-old daughter, were brought to us, and together we were sealed for time and all eternity as a family.

That afternoon, the Bishop threw a party for us at his house and many people from the ward came to congratulate us. Although I had always felt they loved me, I felt I was now more accepted as one of them.

Through it all, I tried to be happy and tell myself that this was really God's way, that the Mormon Church is really God's church. But in the back of my mind, nagging doubts kept nipping at the edges of my joy. After a few days, I managed to convince myself that my thoughts about the ceremony being evil were just Satan working to get me to quit the Mormon Church. Satan was always trying to prevent people from becoming Mormons. That is what the Mormon missionaries had told me. I knew it must be true because I had heard many stories of people who had to fight off terrible events in order to be baptized or enter the temple. I convinced myself again that the Mormon Church was indeed the only true church of God on the face of the earth, and that the more I went to the temple, the more comfortable I would feel with the ceremony. My nervousness, I told myself, came because it was new and different; it would pass with time and familiarity.

I went to the temple many times after that initial visit hoping that familiarity would drive out the terrible feelings I continued to have each time I entered that place. I never became comfortable with the ceremony that smacked so dramatically of cultism. Although I was able to suppress my feelings and get through the ceremony each time, my soul rebelled until I was out of the temple and on my way home.

Several years later I would return to those doubts and recognize them as valid feelings. It was a great disappointment to me to discover that the god the Mormons worship is not a God of love, of inclusivity, who bases his love for us on nothing more than that we are his creation. Rather, the Mormon god is one who plays games with our faith, letting us into heaven based on whether we remember the secret password—sort of like the old Groucho Marx game show on a grander scale. Suddenly, the words of the bishop who had married Dee and me on a beautiful day in 1969 came back to whisper in the depths of spirit: "Do you know what you're getting into?"

FOOTNOTE ON THE TEMPLE CEREMONY: In 1990, the General Authorities of the church changed the temple ceremony significantly. They eliminated the blood oaths or penalties for revealing the signs. Women now take an oath of obedience to God, just as the men do, rather than an oath of obedience to their husbands. The most significant change, for me at least, was the removal of that portion of the ceremony in which religious leaders of other faiths are made to appear as pawns of Satan. Obviously, other people were as offended as I was at such implications. At the veil, no embrace on the Five Points of Fellowship is required, just a simple "left arm upon right shoulder." The changes deleted about two thousand words from the original temple ceremony, including the Lecture at the Veil, according to an article appearing the *Salt Lake City Messenger*, a publication of the Utah Lighthouse Ministry.

Changes to the temple ceremony have raised questions in the minds of many Mormons about the validity of the ceremony in the first place. Mormons were taught for years that the ceremony is a crucial step along the path to the Celestial Kingdom. For several generations faithful Mormons have been taking the blood oaths and hearing the ceremony in the same way. They were told the ceremony reflected God's revealed truth to Joseph Smith, who first implemented the temple ceremony. All Mormons believe that God's revealed truth is the "same yesterday, today, and forever" and cannot be altered. The changes in the ceremony, however, make it obvious that the ceremony came from man, since men have taken so many liberties to alter it. It is one more hurdle of many with which faithful Mormons must struggle in attempting to understand their changing church, after years of being assured that the truth never changes.

2

৪০৪

The Journey Begins

My husband, Dee was the first Mormon I'd ever known. I grew up in a rural area of northern Kentucky near Cincinnati, Ohio. Although I later discovered there were Mormons in our community, I had never been exposed to them or their religion. My husband was what is called in Mormonese a "jack" Mormon, one who is still a Mormon in name, but does not practice to the letter all of the rules of the Mormon Church. For him meant he was a social drinker of alcohol and coffee, two very strict Mormon taboos.

We met through our jobs with a company in Cincinnati, where I was a customer service manager, and he was an electronics technician. He was twenty-two and just out of the Marine Corps, slender, and just under six feet tall with dark wavy hair and a thick mustache that gave him almost a Tom Selleck look. His sense of humor captured me first, and his quick wit told of an intelligence that was above average. He had gone to Cincinnati to visit his sister after his discharge from the Marines, and had then decided to stay for awhile before going back to his native Utah.

His childhood had been traumatic. He was the second of four children. When he was twelve, his mother committed suicide, leaving him, his older sister, and two younger brothers to live with his father and a stepmother who had not bargained for four children to rear. There was no love on the part of the stepmother, and in response to her attitude, their father beat all the kids regularly. Although the family was Mormon, from good pioneer stock, Mormon family values had long deserted this group. Dee's sister married young and moved to Cincinnati where her husband worked at a school for the blind. Dee struggled to find himself, and at age seventeen he joined the Marine Corps. There, he passed a three-year college equivalency test and entered the air wing where he received training at two top Naval electronics/avionics schools. After a tour in Vietnam—where he was wounded twice—he returned to the United States. That life is a constant battle was something he understood early.

I was twenty-one, divorced from my high-school sweetheart, with a three-year-old son. If Dee had seen the darkest sides of life, I had been reared in Utopia. Born of middle-class parents who tried to give their children everything, I experienced a stable, peaceful childhood. I was naive enough to believe everyone lived like our family. Surrounded by an extended family of grandparents, aunts, uncles, and cousins, I felt closely the bonds of that togetherness. Church every Sunday was mandatory, and we attended as a family. My grandparents and others of my extended family went to the same church.

By the time I had reached my twentieth birthday, I had experienced the pain of relationships. It was a young age to have already married, borne a child, and divorced. Life had hit me squarely between the eyes, and I had only begun to find my own path. I had a sense that it would not be easy, but then I met Dee and fell in love.

Though I had been born and reared in the Disciples of Christ (Christian) Church, and my church life was very important, little matters at that age, especially religious preferences. even To me, Dee was just a young, handsome, intelligent man who was a good lover, and a wonderful father to my son. That was really all that mattered. So we decided to get married.

Although he was a jack Mormon, Dee wanted us to be married by the Mormon bishop of a ward in Cincinnati where his sister attended church. They had been reared in Utah so their Mormon roots ran deep in spite of the fact they no longer lived in Zion, the name given to Utah where the Saints or Mormons predominantly live.

It did not take me long to become intrigued by Mormonism. Perhaps my religious upbringing prompted my fascination with religious theology, as well as the sociology and psychology of religion in general. Even as a teenager, I had loved religious history and biblical studies. Although my Christian background was relatively liberal, my parents were quite conservative. I had been reared in a strict manner when it came to things such as church attendance. Still, I did not intend to become a Mormon.

One day while talking to my own minister about my upcoming marriage to a Mormon man, he said to me, "You'll join the Mormon Church someday."

His statement took me aback. "No I won't. Why would I do that," I asked, rather shocked at his statement. "I'm happy with this church."

"You'll join because you have a lot of questions, and Mormons have all the answers," he replied.

His words, as it turned out, were prophetic.

A year later, Dee and I moved to Lorain, Ohio, where he worked for the Federal Aviation Administration as an air traffic controller at the Cleveland center. It was my first move away from home, family, and my horses—everything I'd grown up with, knew, and loved. Sure, I loved Dee, but the move was devastating to me.

We moved into an apartment across the street from Lake Erie. My life became one of grief, loneliness, and fear of the unknown. I went on days-long crying jags and was certain my heart would break from homesickness. I missed the farm. I missed my horses terribly. My center had been ripped away, and I thought I could not survive. Out of my element, I felt frightened and unsure of my future. I finally asked Dee if we could find a Disciples of Christ Christian Church somewhere close by for me to attend. He said church was fine, but he wanted to go to a Mormon Church. Since our move he had become my entire support system—both emotionally and financially—so I conceded. The following Sunday, I looked up the address of the local Mormon ward meeting house[6] where the congregation met and called for directions and meeting times. For the first time, Dee and I went to church together, and I experienced my first encounter with the alien world of Mormonism.

I want to say here and now that whatever else the Mormon people are, whatever dogmatic shortcomings the theology may have, they are undoubtedly some of the friendliest people on the face of the earth. Of course they have an ulterior motive, an underlying and self-serving agenda of winning more converts for the church. I would later learn how often their friendliness is conditional, as is their love and acceptance. They immediately let me know that they wanted us—meaning me, since Dee was already a member—to become a part of them. Conversions to

---

6   Mormons call the place where their individual congregations meet a "meeting house." A ward is a geographic area usually made up of about three hundred people. Each ward has a designated meeting house where Sunday worship services and other meetings are held. Sometimes two or three wards share a meeting house, each ward meeting at a different time.

legalistic religious groups are often easiest when a person's life is in turmoil, and I certainly fit that criteria at that time.

In their book, *The Mormon Murders*, Steven Naifeh and Gregory White Smith interviewed Mark Hoffman, who is serving time in prison for the bombing deaths of his business partner and another partner's wife, over the selling of forged "historical" church documents to Mormon Church leaders. Mark Hoffman, as a young missionary-in-training, was told that church research showed the best prospects for conversion were "blue collar, lower-class workers unhappy with their station in life, and those whose 'ramparts were broken. Your rampart is your circle of friends and your sense of a coherent life,' explains a former missionary. 'When people move, change jobs, get divorced—their ramparts are broken, and that's when they're most susceptible to conversion. Those were the people they told us to go after.'"[7] I was a prime target. I was a lost lamb, and the Mormons offered a fold.

Since my own experience, I have met several acquaintances who also converted to Mormonism at a time when their lives were in upheaval. One friend, a non-Mormon whose wife was a jack Mormon, completely turned his life around by converting to Mormonism shortly after the accidental death of their five-year-old son. His wife became an active member once again, and they were eventually married in the temple with the promise and hope of raising their son in the next life.[8] Mormons seem to offer friendship, comfort, and, more importantly, definitive answers to life's most troubling questions at times when people need all of those things to cope.

---

7   Naifeh, Steven and Smith, Gregory White, *The Mormon Murders*, pg. 67, Wiedenfeld & Nicolson, publishers, 1988.

8   Mormon doctrine teaches that when a child dies, the parents will be permitted to finish raising that child in the Celestial Kingdom, the highest degree of what Mormons believe to be three degrees of heaven.

From the moment we walked through the door of the meeting house, we were surrounded by warmth and love as I had never known before. Not even the people of the church in which I had grown up reacted to strangers the way these people did. I was overwhelmed with kindness, and for a young woman far away from home for the first time, trying to make a new life with a new husband among strangers, being in that Mormon chapel was like coming into a warm, cozy room out of a driving rainstorm. My first encounter with Mormons was overwhelmingly positive, over the next ten years, and it would get better before it got worse.

Conversion is the first and foremost goal of Mormons. When it comes to converting people, and solidifying and maintaining those conversions, nobody does it better than they do. Their "every member a missionary" program coupled with a large, formal missionary system obtains phenomenal results that have allowed the church to grow from its meager beginnings one hundred and fifty years ago to more than ten million members worldwide today. The September 1993 issue of Ensign magazine, the church's officially sanctioned publication, reported that during a five-year period from 1988—1992, 1,478,588 converts were baptized into the church.[9]

The total number, cited by the church, of Mormons worldwide is a figure that can be misleading, however. The number does not take into account the fact that people also leave the church, become inactive, or are excommunicated. I once tried to find out whether or not the church removes from its rolls ex-members or members who no longer participate actively in the life of the church. The nice young lady at the church office in

---

9   In 1988, 256,515 were baptized; 1989, 318,940; 1990, 330,877; 1991, 297,779; and in 1992, 274,477. There is no way to account for the drop-off in baptisms in 1991 and 1992 after a record high in 1990, considering that the numbers of missionaries reportedly in the field are increasing.

Salt Lake City seemed surprised by my question. "Oh," she replied, "No one quits the church." Although the church does not recognize that anyone leaves its ranks, a study on Utah Mormons in the *Journal for the Scientific Study of Religion*, said, "Disaffiliation from fast-growing religious organizations has received comparatively little research attention. Yet, all groups do experience some loss of membership either through members leaving to join other religions or through their termination of formal religious involvement altogether."[10]

The authors of the study went on to say, "The more typical pattern of disaffiliation for Mormons is to 'drop out' of religious participation altogether." Their study revealed that of Mormons who left the Mormon Church, forty-two percent claim "no preference" of religion or "drop outs." Of the remaining fifty-eight percent who left Mormonism to switch to another religion, twenty-two percent switched to Catholicism.

One reason for the high percentage of Utah Mormons to become disaffiliated rather than join another church, say the authors, is that "quiet disaffiliation is easier in a state where three-fourths of the population is Mormon than to joining some visible and status-deviant affiliate with a minority denomination. To join another denomination is to publicly reveal one's apostasy from Mormonism, while remaining disaffiliated with any religion is safe, and leaves one in an ambiguous, and hence less deviant status." Another reason, said the authors, is Mormonism has all truth—other denominations are an inadequate means to salvation and God. "Hence, a neutral, nondenominational position may be more compatible with the

---

10   Albrecht, Stan L., professor of sociology, and Bahr, Howard M., director of Family Resources at Brigham Young University; *Journal for the Scientific Study of Religion*, 1983, Vol. 22, issue 4, pg. 366-379.

values of the former Mormon than affiliation with another denomination."[11]

I later learned that even those excommunicated from the church are not removed from the membership rolls, just moved from one side of the ledger to the other (probably right to left). They are considered to be "apostate" members, but members nonetheless, which accounts for the fact that the church's numbers always show an increase.

The church's growth is a direct result of its worldwide, structured missionary system which is unlike any other religion's. Young men, at age nineteen, and young women, if they have reached the age of twenty-one and are unmarried, receive a "calling" to go on a mission. The calling, which can be to any part of the world, is for a two-year period for young men and eighteen months for young women. (Mormons believe that it is more important for women to marry than to go on a mission.) The first stop is Brigham Young University, where for two weeks the young people receive training and instruction on how to teach the gospel to potential converts. Those called to missions in foreign countries attend BYU's foreign language school for an eight-week crash course in the necessary language, along with conversion instructions. So effective is the school that men who have served on church missions are in high demand for positions as sales personnel with insurance, securities, and other hard-sell companies. Mormon males who serve in foreign countries are often in demand by such agencies as the FBI and CIA because of their fluent foreign language skills, knowledge of foreign cultures, and their perceived high degree of honesty and integrity. The illusion of integrity, however, is one misperception that often comes back to haunt both the church and the individuals involved.

---

11   Ibid.

An August 22, 1990, newspaper article details the trial of former FBI agent Richard Miller, an excommunicated Mormon, who claimed that Mormons in the FBI used religious dogma (i.e., multiple wives are acceptable in the next life, so why not get a head start now) to pressure him into having an affair with a spy from the former Soviet Union. Miller was the only FBI agent ever tried for espionage. He testified that in 1984 Richard Bretzing, then head agent at the FBI's Los Angeles headquarters and a bishop in the Mormon Church, asked him to confess to the indiscretion. Miller had been excommunicated from the church for adultery. He testified that he viewed Bretzing and a fellow FBI agent and Mormon, Phillip Christiensen, as "spiritual advisers" to whom he could tell his troubles. Miller was arrested on October 2, 1984, and charged with giving secret documents to a then-Soviet agent and her husband in exchange for $65,000 cash and sex. Miller spent five years in prison and was released in December 1989.

Like the rest of us, Mormons are only human and subject to moral failings despite all the church's public-relations hype to the contrary. However, as missionaries these young men in their white shirts, ties, and dark suits, present the perfect picture of Mormonism to those with whom they come in contact.

Typically, the missionaries spend much of their time "cold calling" by knocking on doors, seeking out those interested in what they have to say. However, they depend a great deal on local ward members to give them "referrals," or names of friends and relatives who might be interested in taking the "lessons," a series of seven instructional periods designed to bait, hook, then reel in converts. Making converts for the church is the number one goal of Mormon missionaries. I have heard many stories about contests sponsored by the area leaders to encourage competition among the missionaries under their jurisdiction to see who can get the most baptisms in a month. Promises of big steak dinners at local steak houses sound pretty good to these young men whose Spartan missionary lifestyle doesn't often allow for such luxuries. (Missionaries are supported by their families, which means most live sparingly on meager allowances.) Publicly, the church denies that this practice takes place, but many returned missionaries tell stories of the strong competitiveness that serves as an effective way to add numbers to what is already the fastest-growing church in the world. Unlike many other denominations in which the goal is to save souls or build social programs to assist people as a community, the intent of the Mormon missionary program is to increase the membership rolls of the church. The pressure brought to bear upon these young men and women to "make converts" encourages this kind of competition, regardless of whether it is sanctioned by church officials.

When the missionaries came knocking on our apartment door shortly after our first visit to church, I was adamant in my position that I had did not intend to convert to Mormonism. I was strong in my faith and beliefs, or so I thought, and was certain that nothing they said could possibly sway me into joining Mormonism. The question I am asked most often when people find out I was a Mormon for more than ten years is how, with my strong religious background and intelligence, I could believe all that the missionaries told me. My only answer is to repeat what my former minister told me: Mormons have all the answers. It is difficult to argue or debate religion with them unless you know exactly the position from which they are coming; unless you know Mormonism from the inside out there seem to be no arguments to refute their dogma.

I found out that evening that not only do Mormons have all the answers, they know how to ask all the right questions. Remember, they do their missionary work after going through one of the best salesmanship schools in the country. They are trained to phrase questions so that "no" is never an option.

("Wouldn't it be wonderful if you could spend eternity with your family?" Most people could hardly say no to such a question.) As thoroughly as I knew my Bible, that knowledge was of little help to me when faced with these two handsome, smiling, seemingly knowledgeable, impeccably dressed young men. Although they were not any older than I was at the time, they intimidated me with their authoritative "priestly" manner, something I would later learn that keeps many women in their place. Additionally, they taught early Mormon history and taught primarily from the Book of Mormon, both of which were new to me. That made any debate with them impossible, which is the purpose of their teaching style. As a result, I agreed to take the lessons to make my husband happy and to satisfy my own curiosity about the Mormon religion.

The lessons are established in such a way that by the seventh lesson period a person should be ready to make the commitment to baptism into the Mormon Church. During this time, one is encouraged to read the five-hundred-page Book of Mormon from cover to cover, then pray about its "truthfulness." It is crucial to obtain a "testimony" of the Book of Mormon's authenticity as scripture as well as a testimony that Joseph Smith was a "true" prophet of God.

One of the first things that struck me as I became acquainted with the religion was how frequently Mormons used the words "true" or "truth." Knowing for a certainty the "truthfulness" of the whole Mormon gospel is a crucial prerequisite to becoming a member. My later studies in Mormonism taught me just how deeply ingrained this idea of "truth" is. In the hearts and minds of Mormons, the Church of Jesus Christ of Latterday Saints is the only true church of God on earth, and the only one with the entire truth of the gospel.

Bruce R. McConkie, now deceased but long considered the foremost authority on Mormon doctrine during his career as a general authority of the church in Salt Lake City, says in his book, *Mormon Doctrine*, that "True religion, the religion of Jesus Christ . . . is found only in the Church of Jesus Christ of Latter-day Saints. False religion—made up of fragments of truth mixed with error—is found in the Christian sects and among pagan worshipers. There is no salvation in false religion."

When I discovered this statement later in my journey through Mormonism, I was appalled and offended that Mormons could negate so easily the basic tenets of my faith, implying that my Christian upbringing had somehow been "false." In my heart, I knew that wasn't logical thinking, and those statements by McConkie added more fuel to my doubts.

This whole idea of truth—a "true" church—bothered me. To many Mormons faith in Jesus Christ is an ambiguous ideal, whereas they know that proof exists that Joseph Smith lived, saw God and Jesus Christ, and established the church, which constitutes something like scientific proof that Mormonism is true. I grew up believing that faith has less to do with any actual, provable "truth" than with a belief in things not seen. To Mormons, however, having "truth" is everything—truth as they see it, that is.

In the *Doctrine & Covenants*, a book of the writings and personal revelations of Mormon Church founder Joseph Smith, it says, "Truth is absolute and eternal, it endureth forever." (1:39, 88) "It never varies; what is true in one age is true in every age."

This, I would learn later is not necessarily the case even for the Mormons themselves, who have altered many of the original "truths" of Mormonism to accommodate the "outside" Christian world and become accepted as Christians, or to adapt the church to societal changes. That's one of the advantages of having a living prophet—he can alter the truth as he sees fit and create a new truth as necessary to accomplish the aims of the church or prevent disaster within the church. (One example is the case of granting black men the priesthood, which I am convinced was done to avert picketing and possible riots on Temple Square in downtown Salt Lake City during that particularly volatile time).

Much of the strength of Mormonism comes from its members' belief that it is the only "true" church of God on the face of the earth. This Mormon belief, above all other teachings in Mormonism, brings a cohesiveness and profound dedication to Mormonism that is found in few other Christian-oriented religions. Only in the cult infrastructure does such exclusivity capture the hearts and minds of believers to this extent. Unfortunately, I would not understand this until many years later.

The time was nearing for my decision to convert to Mormonism. Several aspects of the religion disturbed me, yet I dared question only one: the church's stance on birth control. Knowing that the Mormon families I had met so far consisted of many children, I was skeptical and worried that perhaps Mormonism was much like Catholicism when it came to issues such as birth control. To get the straight scoop, I went to the bishop and asked him about the church's position on the matter. He informed me that the official stance of the church is that it is a private matter between a woman, her husband, and God. I would find out in a few years that the official position and the "unofficial" pressure that comes from a woman's husband or the church were two very different things.

The fact that I was required to be re-baptized also bothered me. At age nine, I had been baptized by immersion for remission of sins, and I believed that was the one and only baptism I needed. Although Mormons baptize by immersion, which coincided with my belief about the style of baptism, they do not baptize for remission of sin, which is something that disturbed me from a Christian theological standpoint. Mormon baptism is a rite that gives one entrance as an official member in the church, nothing more and nothing less. That was not part of my belief system. Dee, who held the highest office in the Aaronic priesthood—a Priest—baptized me.[12]

The baptism ritual created a nice family togetherness scene, but it was only the beginning of what was to be a long trek through my own personal wilderness. Though I said nothing at the time, I resented the missionaries' comments that my previous baptism was somehow "wrong" and therefore the process had to be redone "right." The idea that life outside the Mormon Church is wrong but that life within it is right still bothers me.

Years later, I cut out a cartoon showing two little funny-looking fellows talking. One says to the other, "Life is very uncomplicated if you just remember one simple rule . . . WE are always right and THEY are always wrong!" It would be one of the most beneficial lessons I was to learn about being a Mormon.

To allay my doubts, the missionaries told me to get on my knees and pray until, as it says in the Book of Mormon, I received confirmation of the truth of Mormonism by a "burning" in my "bosom," reflecting the approval of the Holy Ghost of the step I was about to take. Then I would know for certain, they said, that their doctrine was true.

Well, I tried. I prayed until I had carpet-layer's knees, but I felt nothing like a burning in my bosom. In fact, all that really arose in my inner being were continued feelings of doubt. However, by the time the missionaries arrived for the final lesson and

---

12   There are two priesthood categories in the Mormon Church, the lesser priesthood, the Aaronic, and the greater priesthood, called the Melchizedek priesthood, named after an Old Testament priest. All worthy Mormon males are initiated into the Aaronic priesthood at age thirteen, and then receive the Melchizedek at age nineteen upon being commissioned to go on a mission, or sometimes later as in the case of adult converts.

to set my baptism date, I had convinced myself that this was something I should do in spite of my feelings to the contrary.

It seems strange to me now as I look back on it from a period of nearly thirty years, that although in my heart I knew it was not right for me, I consented to be re-baptized. At that point I would have joined the church no matter what I felt. The pressure was on, and I believe I knew even then that all the love and kindness Dee and I were shown by the members and missionaries was contingent on my baptism, on my becoming one of them.

I've talked to many "converts" in the intervening years, and many tell the same story of their feelings just prior to taking that big step and converting to Mormonism: a feeling comes over them that it's something they shouldn't do, but for some reason, they want to believe it's right. If these doubts are expressed, the missionaries usually say that Satan is creating doubts because the one goal of the Prince of Darkness is to prevent Christians from joining the "true" church. Besides, I wanted to believe, because I thought it would make Dee happy if I became a Mormon, and God knows I was conditioned to want to make people happy. We believe what we want to believe, and our beliefs become our reality. Mormonism became my reality.

3

❧

Becoming Worthy

No single category of people in the Mormon Church is treated better and with more tender, loving care than the "convert," a term that becomes a label, which sticks forever in defining one's relationship to the church. Technically, converts have no greater or fewer rights or opportunities than those born into the church. What sets converts apart is an almost revered or privileged status among those born Mormon. I was always introduced as a "convert," which seemed to entitle me to a special kind of respect. Whereas most Mormons born into the faith tend to take each other and their religion for granted, converts, who come into the fold from the outside, are carefully nurtured and tended, lest they somehow lose faith in the church and fall away. The greatest curse to the church are those "apostates" who have left the church, or "fallen away," as the church likes to put it, and then maligned it by writing or speaking about Mormonism, its doctrines, and its practices, something church leaders find deplorable.

Converts also receive much care and attention because their conversion is an affirmation of the beliefs of those born into

Mormonism, a confirmation of the truthfulness of the Mormon Gospel. That outsiders from other religions choose to join the Mormon religion and give testimony of its truthfulness reinforces the belief structure of those who might tend to take lightly their lifelong membership in the church.

Everyone who is active in the Mormon Church is *very* active.

Part of the church's ability to hold on to its members results from the way that it keeps them busy and involved in the day-to-day life of the church. Everyone has a "calling." Except for the highest General Authority positions, which are based in Salt Lake City, the church is run at all levels by members acting in non-paid, lay-leadership positions. As a result, there is plenty for everyone to do. Converts experience instant involvement and receive a "calling"[13] almost immediately after baptism. My first calling was as assistant organist for the ward chapel. I played when the regular organist was out of town or engaged in other activities in the church.

After a few weeks, I was also called to help in Primary, the children's program that meets once a week for games, crafts, and religious lessons, and which is usually run by the women of the church. The jobs given new converts are mostly innocuous ones in positions where they can be instructed and tutored until they understand Mormonism enough to be a teacher or serve in leadership positions. Male converts are often called to positions with the Boy Scout program, which is heavily promoted in the Mormon Church.

I agree with the Mormon philosophy of using lay people to operate the church at the grassroots level—to a certain point.

---

13   In Mormonism, people are not merely asked to do a job or given a position, but are called by the bishop of the ward, who is said to be acting for God. After a person accepts a calling (very few callings are refused), they are then "set apart" with a blessing by the laying on of hands by the bishop and his two counselors.

In the congregation of the Disciples of Christ (Christian) Church where I had been reared, there had been so much infighting over preachers, hiring and firing of personnel, and power struggles among members, that by age sixteen, I'd become disillusioned with organized religion. Everyone wanted to be paid for whatever they did, be it playing the piano or preparing the communion. I had become disgusted with the way people who called themselves Christians acted.

It was a refreshing change to be part of a church in which everyone accepted the ward's spiritual leader—the bishop. In the Mormon ecclesiastical hierarchy, those who are at the next highest level "call" the bishop. Their decision is approved by the General Authorities in Salt Lake City. The members believe that God calls their bishops, and a member who does not like it is considered out of step spiritually. Likewise, the bishop's two counselors, organists, choir directors, and teachers at the local ward level are also called to these positions. They are then "set apart," a process in which two elders in the ward lay their hands on the person's head and pray for them to be diligent in their calling. While there are some problems that can arise when laymen are used in positions of high authority—which I will address later—overall, people are far more cooperative when they believe they have been called by God to share their talents, rather than hired by a congregation and paid for their work.

Their callings keep Mormons busy and active in the life of the church, something many Protestant denominations seem to have trouble accomplishing, as evidenced by the shrinking membership of many mainline congregations. Mormon Churches might have a tendency to overwork their members, but their method of immediately pulling converts into the life of the church pays off in long-term benefits. In fact, it was the peace and harmony that I experienced in the ward in Lorain, Ohio, that was the main factor in convincing me to join the church.

The other appealing factor that contributed to my becoming a Mormon was that Mormonism provided me a box in which to live. The box was simply a set of rules and regulations, laid out in black and white, that made life easier, freed me from decisions and kept me out of the gray areas of life where making choices was often difficult for me. A road map on which there is only one road, Mormonism tends to break life down into the most simple of terms: right and wrong. Although that may sound good and the lifestyle is certainly easy, as I will discuss later, the theology is problematic.

Dee and I were surrounded by our newfound Mormon friends much like certain species of animals surround the young and weak when threatened by predators. This group quickly became our entire support system, both socially as well as religiously. It did not take me long to learn to cling fiercely to my newly adopted religion and the security it promised me if I obeyed its laws and practiced its tenets faithfully. Lacking in self-discipline, at age twenty-one, I found a comfortable place in which to nest within Mormonism's barriers, which kept me from the uncertainty of the world and kept the outside world from touching me.

In the early days of my membership, there was a time when I would have defended the church and its teachings with my life. The year we spent in Lorain, Ohio, was a year that would change my life—totally and completely for the good. I settled in, put on blinders, and became dedicated to one thing: becoming worthy to enter a Mormon temple with Dee and to be married for time and all eternity. "Worthy" is word that is used often in Mormonism. In a structured, legalistic religion such as Mormonism, whether or not one is worthy to perform various tasks or take on leadership responsibilities is easily determined by one's obedience to the rules and regulations, which act as a yardstick by which one can be measured. Obedience, I quickly learned, is designed to make one worthy in the eyes of God and church officials (mostly the latter) and permits one to move on to bigger and better things, such as entering one of the many temples scattered regionally in the United States and in countries worldwide. I quickly realized that entering the temple was considered the ultimate Mormon experience, one to be coveted by those Mormons who were "unworthy" and cherished by those who had been found worthy enough to pass through the sacred portals, where "secret" rituals forever seal one's afterlife destiny.

So I began pursuing the path toward worthiness. It really was not very difficult, especially for one who had had a rather strict Christian upbringing. Regular church attendance was a must, as was tithing, which in the Mormon Church consists of paying one-tenth of one's gross (not net) income. Those requirements had been a part of my early Christian upbringing, so I had no difficulty obeying. Service in the church in some capacity, such as teaching or leading lessons or singing in the ward choir, was also considered when trying to obtain a "temple recommend," the official permission slip signed by the stake president[14] which allows one to pass through the sacred temple doors. Obedience to all the rules is required, particularly the Word of Wisdom (no tea, coffee or alcoholic beverages).

Obedience, complete and unquestioning, is a key factor in being a good Mormon. Yet, it was something I had always had a problem with as a child and young adult. The firstborn of my family, I was the adventurous one, the daredevil, the one who decided that the thrill of doing what one was told not to do was worth the risk of getting caught. I felt that doing what was considered "different" or weird—off the beaten track—I feel

---

14   A stake president presides over the stake or group of wards and has counselors from the various wards to assist him.

makes life more interesting. If an authority figure told me to do something, I would always ask "why?"

Growing up in the era of the sixties when the societal mores of the United States seemed to have turned upside down, I also became more liberal in my thinking on matters of sexuality and religion. Becoming a Mormon and desiring temple marriage meant forsaking that way of independent thinking. It meant aligning my thoughts, my beliefs, and my behaviors with those of good Mormons everywhere and learning to follow obediently in a path I was told would lead me to the highest degree of Mormon heaven—the Celestial Kingdom. But it was something I was willing to do at that time for the privilege of entering the temple in this life, and the Celestial Kingdom[15] in the next—a place all devout Mormons aspire to go after this life. It is there that men who hold the priesthood faithfully in this life get to become a "god" in the next, where they, along with their multitudes of wives, may procreate "spirits" with which to populate other worlds.

In this life, however, only one wife is allowed, and it is to her the man is sealed for time and all eternity. If she should die, he may remarry another in the temple, because after all, he will have many wives in the hereafter. The woman, until recently, was allowed to wed only one husband in a temple marriage. Now accommodations in the rules allow widowed women to remarry in the temple. In early 1994, the church authorities changed the rule concerning temple divorce. Before the change, only women were required to obtain an official temple divorce.

---

15   Mormon doctrine teaches there are three degrees of glory or heaven: the Telestial, Terrestrial, and the Celestial. Only Mormons who have lived such a perfect life that their "calling and election is made sure" get to go to the Celestial Kingdom. The lessor kingdoms are for "good" people in other religions who failed to become Mormons, or for marginal Mormons who did not completely live up to their religion.

Now, men must also obtain a temple divorce before wedding another woman in the temple. (Now, the only question is the one Jesus' disciples asked him two thousand years ago, "In heaven, whose wife will she be?" Only the Mormons discount the answer Jesus gave, that in heaven people are not married, so I imagine the men will draw straws or duke it out over who gets her.)

It was during that first year that I became completely committed to all that Mormonism taught, and if I didn't totally believe everything the night I was baptized, I came to believe Mormon doctrine with all my heart. Nothing, I was certain, could ever move me from that place—nothing except maybe a move to Utah, the heart of the kingdom of the Saints.

4

ಬಿಣ

Welcome to Utah

$\mathcal{A}$ little more than a year after our move to Lorain, Ohio, Dee and I, and my five-year-old son Keith, packed up and moved again, this time to Utah. Dee missed his home state terribly. I understood his feelings after catching my first glimpse of the Rocky Mountains while flying in the right seat of a Piper Cherokee on our cross-country flight, a few months earlier, to meet Dee's family and to see how I would like living in Utah. In spite of the heartache I had felt at moving to Lorain, I was doubly crushed by our leaving. I had grown to love the church there, and the people of the Lorain ward had become my family, almost closer to me than my own family. Still, I was also excited about the prospects of living in Zion,[16] the name Mormons originally gave to their "Promised Land" that others call Utah.

I believed, from hearing people speak of it, that all Mormons in Utah lived a beautiful, idyllic life in a religious Land of Oz where everyone is touched by the spirit of God, who resides

---

16 Zion is a Biblical name given for the place established as the kingdom of
    God on earth where all people will dwell in peace.

in the "holy of holies" room in the top of the Salt Lake Temple, and everyone lives happily ever after. This image of the Mecca of Mormonism is actively promoted and carefully preserved to enhance Utah's public relations value for the many millions of Mormons who flock to their Holy City each year to enjoy the beauty of the area, taste the history of Mormonism, and have their beliefs about the church reinforced by walking the streets Brigham Young laid out. People in the mission field, a term used to describe all areas outside Utah, long for the day when they can visit Utah to stand in the shadow of the original Salt Lake Temple and visit the Mormon Tabernacle. Inside, the famed Mormon Tabernacle Choir delivers its inspirational message in song each Sunday to the far-flung reaches of the world.

Much of the imagery that the church conveys to the outside world is that of a place full of beautiful, happy people living the perfect family life, the result of their faithfulness to the Mormon Church. It is a picture the church sold to me and one it continues to market to the world via slick magazine and television advertisements. It is really nothing more than public relations hype, as I would learn later, but, it works, as their conversion rates prove. Yet, the church is quite sensitive to public relations, something that has been a challenge during the past decade.

Kaysville is a small town midway between Salt Lake City and Ogden, Utah, just east of Interstate 15. In many ways, it was the most beautiful place I had ever lived. In 1971, there were fewer than ten thousand people living there. Other than a few intersection stop signs, the town had no traffic signals, because there was very little traffic then. It was typical Small Town, U.S.A. One major thoroughfare, appropriately called Main Street, was lined with small shops, a drug store, a movie theater that showed second run PG-rated movies, city hall, and the town's library. The remaining buildings included a bank, two grocery stores, an elementary school built in the 1920s, and the Davis County

High School. If a Utopia could be found on earth, it would have been Kaysville at that time. The town snuggled up against the foot of Francis Peak, a ten-thousand-foot mountain, which is part of the Wasatch Range running north and south from Idaho to southern Utah. In the ten years we lived there, I never tired of the scenery, and today I receive just as much delight in returning to drink in the beauty of that area.

Our move to Utah opened a whole new world for me, a world in which every aspect of life is permeated with the Mormon religion. The whole social and political structure of Utah is steeped in the ideologies of Mormonism, so that the religion lies like an all-encompassing mist over the land. Everyone—Mormon, jack-Mormon, and non-Mormon alike—breathes, eats, and drinks the religion, whether they want to or not. The local media gives non-Mormons subtle daily infusions of the religion, until even the most unconcerned of them become drawn into the issues and conflicts of the state's almost theocratic system. Mormonism, if you live in Utah, is not a religion that can be ignored even though the recent population in-migration, from states like California, has caused a dilution of the Mormon population in Salt Lake City, with non-Mormons now out numbering Mormons.

Life in Utah, even in 1971, was very slow compared to the scrambling pace of the urban areas from which I had come near Cincinnati and Cleveland, Ohio. I believe that one attitude, more than any other factor, contributed to the slowness of life in Utah then: Not much about this life is taken seriously by good Mormons. After all, the next life is the one that counts. Although the same could be said about people in other religious denominations, its prevalence in Utah seemed more noticeable to me because of the high concentration of Mormons in the society. This life is merely for proving one's worthiness for the next—to prepare for the next life by living every tenet of the

Mormon gospel and doing only those things that can assure one's place in the Celestial Kingdom.

Consequently, there is an entirely different air about Utah, which sets it apart even as we have entered the twenty-first century. It is a place that seems untouched by the world—more so then than today as the world makes plans to rush in for the 2002 Olympic Games. You know when you arrive that you are somewhere unique; a place unlike any you have ever been before. Friends and business associates who go to Utah on skiing vacations and business trips often remark how different everything feels. It is nothing on which they can put their finger, but they notice a definite difference. I have compared it to a "Stepford"-like society where everyone seems to be a cookie-cutter image of everyone else, specifically among the Mormon population. In time, I would learn that the same problems that plague the rest of society also infect Utah Mormon society, but those problems are kept hidden away from the view of the outside world, and even within Mormonism are seldom acknowledged.

Unfortunately—or perhaps fortunately—the 1990s brought much change to the Salt Lake Valley. Many companies opened offices and manufacturing plants in the area, some moving from previous sites in California to take advantage of Utah's business-friendly climate. The coming of the Winter Olympics in 2002 resulted in some changes in Utah's liquor laws to accommodate the social life of the thousands of visitors for that event. Traffic jams, miles of new freeways, and hundreds of new housing developments have taken its toll on a once-quiet way of life.

As I prepared to move to Utah, in July of 1971, many people in the Lorain, Ohio, ward planted various illusions in my head about life in Zion. Many were envious of our move. My friends in Ohio were, I believed, the warmest, friendliest, most honest, and genuinely loving people I had ever met, so I assumed that was the way all Mormons were. I had also come to believe, by that time, that living the Mormon way of life guaranteed one a good life free of the turmoil that afflicts people of the world. I had been taught that complete obedience to all the rules of the church leads one to reap all the rewards of this life without many—if any—of the problems that those outside the church must endure. Paying a full tithe, for example, would free one from financial woes. Favorite stories told often in church meetings are of the good "brother" (Mormons call each other Brother or Sister so-and-so) who was laid off from his work and was down to cashing his last unemployment check. But he paid his full tithe out of the money and, lo and behold, he found a job the next day paying twice what his old job had paid. I listened to these amazing testimonials and came to believe every word. Faith-promoting stories like these, told mostly on Fast and Testimony Sunday,[17] boosted my own belief that perfect obedience to religious laws could lead one to live a perfect life. Perhaps I was naive, (in fact I know I was naive) but I was in awe of these people whose lives seemed so white, so pure, and so perfect that I longed more than anything to be just like them.

I received more attention in Utah than I ever had before. Utah Mormons, mostly born and reared in Mormonism for several generations, adored converts from the mission field. Whereas in the Lorain, Ohio, ward I had been just one of many converts, in Utah, as a convert from the mission field, I was something of an anomaly. I was living proof that their missionary system, to which the church is completely dedicated, works—that their

---

17 The first Sunday of each month, all Mormons fast for a twenty-four-hour period, then give the money they saved on food (usually two meals worth) to a special fund to aid those among them who do not have enough to eat. During the Sunday service, people stand up and bear testimony to the "truthfulness" of the Mormon gospel by relating faith-promoting stories or events that happen in their lives.

sons and daughters, who toil so diligently at great expense to
their parents, are not working in vain. A report issued in 1983 in
the *Journal for the Scientific Study of Religion* said that by 1980, one in
ten adult Mormons were converts. Today that number is much
higher as the success rate for conversions increases. (It is difficult to get official statistics from the Mormon Church. The statistics they provide are usually skewed to favor a success ratio.
There are, for example, no statistics available on the number of
people that leave the church each year.) Every time I rose to
bear my testimony on Fast Sunday, it was further reinforcement
to the people of my new ward that their gospel really is the true
gospel—that they, more than any other religious people on
earth, are accepted and loved by God. They relished hearing my
conversion story, and I reveled in telling it for the attention I received. Always one for dramatics, always the class clown, always
the one craving attention, I was suddenly in a place where I received all the attention I wanted. The notoriety I achieved in
Utah over the years also put me in the spotlight when I began
questioning Mormon doctrine.

Because of my status as a convert I was almost revered
among the ward members. And, early on at least, I was more
readily forgiven if I said something that was not entirely in line
with Mormon doctrine. I was, after all, a "baby" in the gospel
and could not be held accountable for stumbling now and then.
Because I had been raised in a different social setting and with a
different religious belief system, I was always looked upon as
being a bit strange. Speaking my own mind often had gotten me
into trouble when I was growing up at home, and it was something I continued to do on a regular basis. I always gave my opinion, whether it was welcomed or not; that did not change much
after I became a Mormon. Because I was so enthusiastic and so
actively involved in the church, however, my outspokenness
was not troublesome to the priesthood hierarchy until much

later in my Mormon experience. Outspoken women in Utah Mormon society are tolerated, at best, and, at worst, silenced by the priesthood, under whose authority their lives are lived, with threats of being disfellowshipped or excommunicated if they get too vocal on matters of social issues and church doctrine.

I learned this lesson through one of the first close friendships I developed after moving to Kaysville. "Beth" lived near me in the same ward and had seven of the most wonderful children I had ever known. She had an open, loving spirit that allowed her to embrace all people on a very basic and highly spiritual level. Her accepting manner led her to develop friendships outside the church as well. Such friendships are not discouraged by Mormon officials, but there is an unwritten understanding—one of many—that one does not develop friendships with those outside the fold of Mormonism unless it is for the purpose of bringing them into the church. Long-term friendships with non-Mormons are discouraged because of the possibility of being led astray and the fear that too much association with those outside the church poses a threat to Mormons.

Beth, however, had a curious mind when it came to exploring the heights and depths of religion, and she loved to study scripture and doctrine, not just of Mormonism, but of other religions as well. She loved talking with me about the Bible, of which I had a thorough knowledge, and she had discovered in-depth only recently. (Although Mormons profess to believe in the Bible "in so far as it is translated correctly," they teach that it contains many errors and inaccuracies. Mormons are encouraged to put the Book of Mormon first as authentic scripture, therefore, most Mormons know the Book of Mormon extremely well but know very little about the Bible.) Beth was eager to talk to me because of my Christian background, about which she was curious. Eventually—and unfortunately for her—she began questioning Mormon dogma. Perhaps she did not so much question it as try to incorporate those things she was learning from her charismatic Christian friends into Mormon doctrine, something that is a little like trying to mix oil and water.

Meanwhile, I was diving headlong into Mormon doctrine, trying to learn all I could about Mormon history and dogma so I could become as well versed in the Book of Mormon as I was in the Bible. Underlying my ambitions to learn was the knowledge that to be fully accepted as a Mormon in Utah, I somehow had to become a Mormon from the inside out. After all, if one is going to swim in the pond with ducks, one had better look like a duck, act like a duck, and grow feathers. I would learn from experience that Mormonism is a religion that one cannot study too closely or delve into too deeply, because often it creates more questions than it answers. I have known many people, over the past thirty years, who have left the church because they studied the doctrine too deeply and uncovered the many dichotomies that exist. At that point in my life, however, I was determined to become a Mormon through and through, not only to prove my worth to the church but to become completely accepted in Utah Mormon society.

At the time I was steeping myself in Mormon doctrine, my best friend Beth made an amazing discovery: the "grace" of Jesus Christ. She came upon this phenomenon by studying her Bible and from listening to her Pentecostal friends. She knew she had uncovered what she believed to be the real meaning of Christianity. In her enthusiasm and excitement, she began talking extensively about the subject to anyone who would listen. For most "churched" people of the Christian persuasion, talk about grace would not be unusual, but for a Mormon, not only was speaking of the theological ideology of grace unusual, it was practically blasphemous. Grace is not a part of Mormon dogma and is rarely mentioned. I learned this lesson the hard way. The very first time the Lorain ward bishop asked me to address the congregation at a Sunday morning service, I chose the topic of grace, using references from the Apostle Paul's letters. I thought I gave a wonderful sermon or "talk" as Mormons prefer to call it, until I was pulled aside by the bishop and his two counselors after church. They kindly told me that Mormons don't talk about grace, because they believe that people receive salvation and a place in heaven based on their works and obedience to God's law, i.e., Mormon law.

Again, I was taken aback by something that seemed totally inconsistent with Christian theology. At the same time, I was informed that Mormons do not refer to themselves as Christians. The term Christian, the bishop explained, was reserved for Protestants and Catholics. Mormons consider themselves totally and completely separate from either of those groups. That offended me too, but as with everything that offended me in those early years, I managed to talk myself out of my doubts and into a stronger belief in all that was Mormon. I never again referred to myself as a Christian until I became friends with Beth.[18]

Not only had Beth found some new Christian friends, she actually attended Wednesday evening prayer meetings with them. She was awed by their openness, their lively singing, and—because it was a charismatic, evangelical congregation—their vibrant activity such as hand clapping, jumping up and down, and even falling in the aisles or being "slain in the spirit" during the service. She also attended their faith-healing services and became very enamored of the group, one of two non-Mormon churches in town. In fact, she was so caught up in

---

18 Now, Mormons want to be referred to as Christians in order to enhance their public image among people of other faiths. However, few Christians are willing to apply that label to Mormons yet.

this group that she began to teach like them. Beth's position as the spiritual development leader in Relief Society[19] gave her the audience and the prime opportunity once a month to teach us about grace and all the other Christian dogmatic ideologies she had discovered at the little charismatic church.

I understood what she was saying because of my familiarity with Christianity, but I knew from my experience in Lorain that this teaching was far afield from what Mormons believed. I was uncomfortable with Protestant fundamentalist doctrine in the first place, and wedged between slabs of Mormonism so that it might pass unnoticed, was a bit much even for my more liberal mind. Beth's strange teachings did not go unnoticed. Other sisters in the ward, who had never heard such things before, found Beth's lessons to be completely incomprehensible. Many wondered aloud what in heaven's name Beth could possibly be thinking. Of course, it was reported to the bishop, and Beth soon found herself being interrogated about her teachings, and her loyalty to Mormonism questioned.

She was censured and told that her spiritual development lessons had to be limited to approved Mormon doctrine taken directly from the lesson book. She was also warned about continuing her relationship with the people who were leading her astray and away from the true gospel into some perverted doctrine that was not approved by church leaders or God. I feared for Beth's church membership, however, that time she received only a warning.

Her husband was also called in for a meeting and told to keep his wife under control, which is the norm. After all, as spiritual head of the household men are responsible for the behavior of their wives. However, Beth was not one to be silent when she had found something in which she really believed, and she was

---

19   Relief Society is the name of the women's organization of the church.

not in the least deterred by the bishop's warning. She and I continued to talk often about the Bible; these many hours of conversation with Beth, during the time we were friends, would eventually take my life full circle.

Over the years since that first incident, Beth has been censured many times, disfellowshipped, and even threatened with excommunication, but in the face of it all she continues—as far as I know—to maintain her friendships with the Christian Protestant community in Kaysville and hold onto her membership in the Mormon Church. She is, however, not allowed to teach or hold any office in the church. Although several of her children have married in the temple, Beth is always denied a recommend because of her unauthorized activities. She continues to this day—as far as I know—to reconcile both of her belief systems and appears to be happy, even though her beliefs force her to live on the periphery of the church in which she grew up and she professes to love so dearly.

Mormon women learn quickly that having one's own thoughts and openly speaking them are two different things. Keeping silent, they learn, is the better part of valor. Over the ten years I lived in Kaysville, many women spoke with me of their true feelings, knowing their thoughts were safe with me. They struggled with the problems of large families and birth control, and other problems created for women by a patriarchal religion. Their trust in me made me feel good—everyone needs someone in whom they can confide honestly. In Utah, it is so difficult to know whom to trust with your innermost thoughts and feelings without fear that they will get back to the bishop.

It was then I began to understand that Mormon women had no voice, no one to speak for them in a society where they dared not speak for themselves. To do so was to risk censure and even excommunication by the priesthood under whose authority they lived their lives. Few were willing to take that risk. I was troubled by this aspect of the religion, but tried to ignore it. Later I would learn why they were so unwilling to speak out.

I was and continue to be deeply saddened by the fact that Utah Mormon society forces many women to live a double life in order to survive in and be part of that society. Sonia Johnson in her book *Housewife to Heretic* calls it having a "split consciousness." Many of my closest friends lived with this split consciousness. Even I experienced that uncomfortable sense of betrayal of one's self that comes from believing one thing and living another in order to be accepted in the society.

Although some men are also outspoken, and even attempt to speak for women, the women are watched more closely and censured more often, probably because men belong to the good ol' boys priesthood club. The priesthood leaders of my ward tolerated me for quite a long time before they began to perceive me as a threat to the conservative role of women in the ward and took steps to silence me.

It was not always this way for Mormon women, however. In the early days of the church when Mormons generally suffered persecution for their beliefs,[20] women were considered spiritual

---

20   Contrary to what many people believe, Mormons did not suffer persecution because of their practice of polygamy. In fact, Mormons did not begin practicing polygamy until later during the Nauvoo days. Joseph Smith began taking other wives without the knowledge of Emma, his first wife. Polygamy was a common practice among many of the religious sects that arose during that period between 1796 and 1830 known as the Second Great Awakening, and took hold in about 1835. The most well-known and longest surviving of these was the sect at Oneida, New York, a commune where "spiritual wifery" was practiced. Another sect led by John Noyes in Putney, Vermont, also practiced polygamy. None of the sects that practiced polygamy were harassed by the general population because during this period people were open to experiment and innovations and "considered it a virtual necessity 'to receive the rays of truth from every quarter . . . changing our views and language and practice as often and as fast as we obtain further information.'" (Charles G. Finney, *Lectures on Systematic Theology,* James H. Fairchild; ed., Oberlin, Ohio, 1878, copyright 1846.)

equals with men in spite of the fact that they could not hold the priesthood. That began to break down after the temple ceremony and polygamy were incorporated into Mormon doctrine. Still, women practiced healing by the laying on of hands[21] and could prophesy.

Eliza R. Snow, one of the most respected women of the early church, a poet and hymn writer, was called a "prophetess" by Smith's successor, Brigham Young. Yet, as the church moved west to Utah and became a more formally organized and structured theocracy under Young's direction, women gradually lost that power. Author Gerda Lerner says, "Women found temporary, often short-lived support for the notion of their innate equality with men as creatures of God in the heretical sects. … In this, they followed a pattern already noted in the history of early Christianity: as long as movements were small, loosely structured and persecuted, women were welcomed as members, given access to organizational leadership and shared authority with men. When the movement became successful, it became more tightly structured, more hierarchical and more male-dominated. Women were then relegated to auxiliary roles and to invisibility."[22]

My first experience with this lack of autonomy for women in the church came very early in my church membership when, in the early 1970s, the general authorities took the formerly independent women's Relief Society and placed it under the auspices of the male priesthood. The more outspoken women

---

21   "At the close of one meeting (of Relief Society) Emma [Smith], Sarah Cleveland, and Elizabeth Whitney laid their hands on the head of Elizabeth Durfee, who was ill and blessed her." Valeen Tippetts Avery and Linda King Newell, *Mormon Enigma, Emma Smith: Prophet's Wife, Polygamy's Foe*, pg. 110; Doubleday, 1984.

22   Lerner, Gerda, *The Creation of Feminist Consciousness*, pg. 74; Oxford University Press, 1993.

of the church showed some resistance, but as usual they were silenced and told that when the Prophet speaks, no one is to question or argue with his authority. Being young in the church, I felt the women were right to be upset, but I never spoke openly about it. At that time, I did not have enough understanding of the issues surrounding women in the Mormon Church to openly take sides.

At first my new membership in the church made me feel accepted and loved, as if I had a whole new family, which in essence I did. Many unfortunate people learn to a greater extent than I did, that often your Mormon family becomes your only family. Although my parents were accepting of my decision to become a Mormon, some people join at the risk of falling out of favor with their families. Mormons work hard at making converts feel a part of their "family," and many people actually shun their families after joining Mormonism. Although in many cases this is neither intentional nor encouraged officially by Mormon authorities, there is an underlying feeling of separateness or exclusivity that comes with one's membership in this group that claims for itself to be the only true church of Jesus Christ. I often get calls from parents whose children have joined the Mormon Church because of a boyfriend or girlfriend, then married in the temple. The feeling that their children have rejected them in favor of the Mormon Church runs deep in these people, and they are hurt by it.

Although I believe that many people in Utah are genuinely good people, the exclusive attitude of Mormonism precludes many of them from feeling loving and friendly to outsiders[23]—even family—or those who fall away into inactivity or are

---

23   In the church's 158th general Conference in 1987, Dallin Oaks, former president of Brigham Young University and former Utah Supreme Court justice and then a member of the council of Twelve Apostles for the church, gave a talk in which he quoted from a letter he had received. The letter com-

excommunicated for violations of church doctrine. Before my
life as a Mormon was over, I would know and feel their wrath
just as deeply and surely as I had known and felt their love.

---

plained that newcomers to Utah who are not Mormons find themselves
"excluded at best and ostracized at worst." An AP news article went on to
say that had been demonstrated the previous week when a Sacramento,
California developer, John Roberts "rejected a job as chief of the private
Utah Economic Development Corp., saying Utah has an image of ostraciz-
ing non-Mormons. Roberts was quoted as saying, 'I was asked what my religion was more in one afternoon in Salt Lake City than I have in my entire
life.'"

5

✂

Mormon Women in Utah: Issues of Birth Control

*W*hen we moved there, Kaysville was, and still is to a large extent, a homogeneous community made up of white, middle class Mormons, a community where one family was pretty much like another and where ninety-nine percent of the people looked alike, thought alike, acted alike, and talked alike. And everyone smiled and appeared happy—too happy. Later in my Mormon experience, I would view Kaysville and its inhabitants as some kind of science fiction movie—a "Stepford" of sorts.

There were no people of color in Kaysville then, except for the occasional Native American child brought to live with one of the middle class, Caucasian families as part of the church's

Indian Placement program.[24] It was not until our family moved
to Arizona some ten years later that my children first saw a black
person.

I often say that when I eventually began turning around and
coming out of Mormonism, I was spiritually bankrupt. As I look
back, I think it was more a matter of having lost my soul. The
shallowness of the people in Kaysville and surrounding communities, and the homogeneousness of the communities gave
life there a flatness. People and life there lacked depth, primarily
because life was one-dimensional. Every aspect of life in Kaysville revolved around the church and church activities. Women
talked about babies, their husbands, food storage, and how to
make the latest great casserole or gelatin salad. Everything and
everyone lacked depth and color, and seemed devoid of
soul—factors that I now know are critical to my own spirituality. Their absence gave me the feeling of spiritual bankruptcy.

The peace and quiet of Kaysville were absolutely addictive,
however. The community seemed almost surreal compared to
the outside world: tree-lined streets, the sounds of children
laughing and playing, neat and tidy homes with manicured
yards, each with a garden in the back. It was a good family town
before the building boom of the 1990s changed the face of
Kaysville. It was a place where people felt safe in their homes.

---

24   The Indian Placement program was created by the church in response to the
      Mormon belief that it had a great responsibility to the Native Americans to
      teach them the "truthfulness" of the gospel, thus fulfilling the promise in
      the Book of Mormon that as the Indians, or Lamanites as they are called in
      that book, are taught and come to accept the gospel of Mormonism, they
      will become a "white and delightsome" people. After much criticism from
      both outside and inside the church, those words were amended in a recent
      edition of the Book of Mormon to read "pure and delightsome." In recent
      years, the Indian Placement program was cancelled, largely due to protests
      from tribal leaders against taking children out of their native culture.

Children could grow up relatively unscathed by the world's evils. And there were children!

The size of the families simply amazed me, not just in Kaysville, but throughout Utah. In June of 1992, a report in the *Christian Science Monitor* said that birthrates in Utah were roughly double that of the national average. The state also had the largest population of people under the age of twenty-five. Burgeoning enrollment put a terrible crush on the public education system. Although large families were not particularly rare when I was growing up, as there was a large Catholic population in the area, never had I lived in a place where there were such swarms of children everywhere. My aunt married a Catholic and had nine children in eighteen years, and I had grown up around these cousins knowing it was Catholicism's teaching against birth control that resulted in this one-family baseball team. But in Utah, there seemed to be an amazing number of children and pregnant women.

I had friends who, it seemed, were perpetually pregnant, whom I could hardly recognize when they were not. Indeed, it did not take me long to realize that being thin and non-pregnant was definitely abnormal in Utah society. I was glad that I was six months pregnant with our first child when we moved to Utah. I fit in well with the overall population, and it helped me gain even greater acceptance in my new home. If converts are revered, pregnant converts are adored. Until I moved to Utah, I never realized the tremendous importance that Mormons place on having children—lots of children. I soon discovered that being pregnant gives Mormon women the highest status they will ever know in Utah Mormon society. One day a friend of mine, who was not much older than I, but who already had four children, remarked to me, somewhat sadly, "The only time I feel good about myself is when I'm pregnant." I remember being struck by a sense of pity for her, and later that was replaced by anger at a church that puts women in a position where their self-worth is directly attached to their ability to reproduce.

At one time in my particular ward, eight of us were pregnant and all due to deliver within a month or so of each other. It became a private joke among us at Relief Society meetings that the priesthood must have spiked the drinking water at church. Although we laughed about it, I knew it was not funny. I believe the other women knew it too, but none of us—not even me—said so at the time.

For all my efforts at being a good Mormon, the one thing I refused to give up was my firm belief in birth control. I was adamant that no one should have to have a child they did not want. However, I did try to stay somewhat in line with Mormon teaching. Before quitting "the pill" to become pregnant with my daughter, I prayed fervently to Heavenly Father (the Mormon expression for God) to reveal to me whether I should have a child. I was twenty-four years of age, and my son was six, so I believed it might be time to have a child with Dee. Three evenings in a row I prayed about this, and three nights in a row I had a very vivid dream in which I had given birth to a beautiful, black-haired daughter. Each night, she was a little older, and more beautiful. I took the hint and told Dee that I thought God wanted us to have a child.

I firmly believe that dreams are a way that our higher power communicates to us and to this day believe she was meant to come to us at that particular time and place. In spite of that, after she was born I went back on the pill. Eventually, Dee and I had two more children, both boys, one in 1974 and another in 1977. Birth control is one of the causes I supported then and to this day. However, what I did not know at the time was that would be a cause that would contribute to my dispute with church authorities and lead to my eventual excommunication from the church.

In 1979, I had my tubes tied. Trying to get a tubal ligation in Kaysville, Utah, was almost as difficult as trying to find a drink of alcohol. (Kaysville had no bars and sold no liquor anywhere.) I went to my family doctor, who had delivered my two sons, and requested he do it.

"You don't want to have your tubes tied," he told me solemnly. "That's against the church's teachings. You're young and healthy and capable of having a lot more children."

"I'm thirty and have all the children I need or want," I told him, getting just a little angry.

"Well, you'll have to find someone else to do it," he replied. "I can't be responsible for the fact that in the next life you won't be able to give birth to any spirit children."

Mormons believe that having our physical tubes tied in this life means eternal sterility in the next. I had received another Mormon theology lesson. I left his office and got an appointment with the doctor, affiliated with the large Hospital in Ogden, who had delivered my daughter. Although he too was a Mormon, he performed the tubal ligation without question, agreeing that I was old enough to know my own mind and decide for myself when enough was enough.

Mormon doctrine teaches that the number of children one has in this life is inextricably intertwined with one's faithfulness to the gospel, obedience to church leaders, and willingness to sacrifice everything for the church. After this life, if one has been faithful to all the commandments, a man and his wife go the Celestial Kingdom, where he will take hundreds more wives, and they will populate the spirit world with thousands of spirit children, who will then in turn be sent to other "Earths" in the form of human beings to populate worlds.

The Mormon vision of "heaven" is a place where thousands of spirits are waiting eagerly for us here on earth to provide bodies for them so they may come to Earth and experience life in a

physical form. Therefore, it is tantamount to a duty—an obligation—for good Mormon couples to have as many children as
they can in order to provide the best possible bodies and home
environment for these spirits. Church leaders repeatedly urge
couples not to postpone or delay having children, as such
actions would place limitations on or delay blessings that God
bestows on couples who take seriously God's command to
"multiply and replenish the earth."

Bruce R. McConkie stated in his book, *Mormon Doctrine*,
"God has commanded his children to multiply and fill the earth,
and the earth is far from full." Just how full Elder McConkie
thought the earth should be I am not certain. Full to the point
that we can no longer sustain life because we have used up all
our resources? I disagreed with that philosophy, however,
most of my female friends in Kaysville took Elder McConkie
seriously.

Many women have large numbers of children out of nothing more than the tremendous guilt placed upon them by the
church if they choose to limit the size of their families. In the
Brigham Young Discourses, the new edition (p. 197), he says,
"There are multitudes of pure and holy spirits waiting to take
tabernacles [bodies], now what is our duty? To prepare tabernacles for them; to take a course that will not tend to drive those
spirits into families of the wicked, where they will be trained in
wickedness, debauchery and every species of crime. It is the
duty of every righteous man and woman to prepare tabernacles
for all the spirits they can."

Joseph Fielding Smith, in a talk given at the October 1965
general conference of the Mormon Church, said, "Now I wish
to ask a question: How will a young married couple feel when
they come to the judgment and then discover that there were
certain spirits assigned to them and they refused to have them?
Moreover, what will be their punishment when they discover

that they have failed to keep a solemn covenant and spirits awaiting this mortal life were forced to come here elsewhere ... I regret that so many young couples are thinking today of successful contraceptives [rather] than of having a posterity. They will have to answer for their sin when the proper time comes and actually may be denied the glorious Celestial Kingdom." He went on to call birth control "this evil practice."

When I discovered that statement, I felt devastated. I was a good Mormon, working diligently in church organizations including Relief Society, Primary, and the Scouting program, and I was being told that because I was practicing birth control, I was the equivalent of a witch or something out of *The Exorcist*. After thinking about Smith's statement, I became angry. How did some old man dare tell women that practicing birth control was "evil!" a "sin!" What business was it of his?

In an article called *The Thirteenth Year in Zion*, Duane Keown, a professor from the University of Wyoming, stated: "More compelling than any long list of theological reasons for having many children is the enormous social pressure brought by membership in the Mormon Church. There is great social satisfaction in being as spiritual as your neighbor, and it brings acceptance in the church."[25]

Because I became actively involved in many of the community events in Kaysville, I had friends all over town, not just in the ward where we attended church. Some my own age, had twice the number of children I had. Most had five or six by age thirty, and many had double that by the time they reached age forty.

If spoken of at all, birth control was a subject that was only mentioned in whispers when we were sure there were no men around. Some of my friends practiced birth control secretly—

---

25   *The Humanist*, July/August 1986, Duane Keown.

even their husbands did not know they were on the pill. Those women who felt the pill was too much a conscious, overt act each day opted for less-obvious methods such as the IUD, which was popular in the 1960s and early 1970s prior to its known dangers. There is also a form of tubal ligation that supposedly can be reversed in which the fallopian tubes are merely bent double and banded rather than completely severed. Knowing that this method is reversible somehow assuages the guilt that Mormon women often feel at permanently curtailing the birth of children.

A friend's daughter had three children in rapid succession. Because she was only twenty-two at the time, she opted for the reversible tubal ligation. Her mother explained to us sisters in a Relief Society meeting one day that her daughter chose this method to give herself a "breather" but really wanted many more children. Many women were actually afraid that the priesthood might find out they did not want more children and never intended to have more, so excuses for birth control—when it was practiced at all—were various and many.

𝔈𝔒𝔒𝔊

Many women in Utah Mormon society who cannot have children, for one reason or another, often feel completely left out of the mainstream of Mormon womanhood; suffer terribly with low self-esteem. If childlessness is difficult for many women in our society as a whole, that feeling is compounded in Utah Mormon society. "Sherry" wanted a baby desperately, but even though she and her husband had been married for ten years they had no luck. She was so envious of every pregnant woman in the ward that I felt sorry for her when one of us got pregnant. She began going to a fertility specialist and would tell us women at Relief Society meetings all the problems she was having. It was beginning to look as if the couple would never have a child of their own. The agony and desperation they went through for so many years was heart wrenching to watch. Finally, after several more years of trying, Sherry and her husband adopted a little girl.

No where in the world are babies wanted more than among Utah Mormons. This opens an opportunity for some enterprising women to operate baby-selling businesses. Several years ago Nelda Karen Colwell was convicted of conspiracy and two counts of aiding and abetting for the smuggling of two Mexican babies into the United States to be sold in Utah. Tried in Laredo, Texas, Colwell, of Layton, Utah, a small town two miles north of Kaysville, received a suspended sentence of three years in prison and a $1,000 fine on each of the two counts. Colwell said she had helped bring more than seventy infants, who were born to impoverished Mexican women, into the United States to be adopted by wealthy Utah couples who were unable to find babies to adopt in this country. The judge who sentenced Colwell said he believed that she was caught up in a "social phenomenon."

In August 1985, a judge gave Deborah Rae Tanner of Wilcox, Arizona, probation after convicting her on sixteen counts of fraud for her part in a Mexican baby-adoption business. She was accused of helping to bilk 180 couples in forty states of $750,000 in a scam that she claimed never made her rich and "barely supported her six children," according to a newspaper report. The victims in this fraud were mostly from Utah (not surprising); a few were from Massachusetts. I knew several women who, like Sherry, who would have paid any price to be able to have or adopt a baby, an attitude that feeds con artists in the baby-selling business and paves the way for fraud.

Even those with only one or two children often feel compelled to offer an explanation about why they only have one or two children instead of eight or nine children. It was always some long story involving complications during pregnancy and a doctor's advice not to have more. I imagined that some of these women (they were very few) really didn't want a large family, but knew it was prudent—in order to preserve their religious integrity—to give medical reasons for their small family size.

Because I bought into the Mormon program for the most part, I, too, came to believe—as most Utah Mormon women believed from childhood—that our salvation lies in our ability to bear children. To be "co-creators with God," as we were so often reminded by church leaders, was our highest and best calling in this life. In spite of the fact that I retained an adamant belief in birth control and family planning, I also wanted the assurance that a very special blessing awaited me from my "partner" in heaven for my obedience in having children. And I felt just a little guilty when I used birth control pills, the words of church leaders echoing in my head.

But that is just one of the many ways the church uses the tremendous weight of being denied the Celestial Kingdom—and never seeing your loved ones and family again—as a whip to coerce people—especially its women—into complete obedience. The thought of some poor, little spirit baby being born into a home of wretched conditions because of the "evil practice" of birth control is more than some women can bear. They sacrifice everything—their health, their personal happiness, and the well-being of their marriage—trying to live up to the impossible "laws" of the church which often have no basis in reality.

Jeff and Sue bought into this program, actually believing that there were a specific number of "spirits" assigned to them for which they were compelled to provide physical bodies. They believed that when parents had the requisite number of children they were assigned, that God would magically turn off the sperm faucet (or the egg faucet) and automatically the baby factory would shut down.

Nine months and one week after their marriage, Jeff and Sue gave birth to a baby girl. I went to visit them, took the baby a present, and asked them about birth control. Perhaps it was really none of my business. Jeff was a good friend and since they were both struggling to finish college, I was concerned about their strapped financial condition and lack of health insurance. They were adamant in their belief that Heavenly Father would take care of the situation. After all, He knew they could not handle anymore children at that time.

Less than one year later, they had another child. Sue had managed to graduate, but Jeff was still a student, and the bills were piling up since there had been no medical insurance to cover either pregnancy. A little more than a year after the second child, they had a third baby. Jeff had graduated and they moved to Kaysville where Jeff was hoping to find a job. In the meantime, Sue became pregnant with their fourth child in less than six years. Sue was very upset and depressed all the time. Her mother came to be with her and, although she, too, was a Mormon, was angry and upset about this rapid succession of grandchildren that was destroying her daughter mentally and emotionally. Every time I tried to talk to them about birth control, they assured me that Heavenly Father would shut the faucet off for sure this time.

To add to their problems, Jeff was having trouble finding a job. I told Jeff I would help him get a job at the manufacturing plant where I was working on one condition: that he practice some form of birth control. Jeff finally admitted that he was ready to use something to prevent another pregnancy, conceding that God did not seem to be doing such a good job in this matter. Although I am sure they suffered their share of guilt about curtailing the birth of more children, Jeff confessed to me some years later that it was the best decision they had ever made. As the children got older, Sue returned to teaching, which she loved, and they finally got their medical bills paid. Today, the children are young adults, and everyone is doing very well.

I felt angry and betrayed by that bishop in Lorain, Ohio, who had told me that birth control was a matter of personal choice, when in reality the doctrine on that subject is quite clear; it is almost identical to the doctrine of Catholicism. I wanted nothing to do with a church that held its women captive by making them fertility slaves. Had I known the truth about Mormons' belief in birth control before joining the Mormon Church, I would never have become a part of a group that did not allow women autonomy over their bodies. (However, outside Utah, things are quite different, and it may have been true that the bishop in Lorain knew only the church's official stance on birth control—that it is a personal matter. That he had never read the comments of church leaders, both past and present, surprised me somewhat.)

The male attitude toward birth control is much like it is in very "macho" countries or countries where there is a rigid patriarchal structure: Lots of children is proof of male virility and/or obedience to the church. Therefore, men are opposed to birth control in any form. One of the most extreme examples of just how important large numbers of children are to the status of priesthood-holding Mormon males, and to what lengths some men will go to protect that status, is the case of Richard Worthington. On September 21, 1991, he took over the maternity ward of Alta View Hospital in Sandy, Utah, at gunpoint, shooting and killing nurse Karla Roth. He was angry because he had discovered that, two years earlier, his wife had "conspired" with her doctor to tie her tubes after their eighth child was born. He went to the hospital to kill the doctor who had performed the surgery. According to newspaper reports, a neighbor of the family said that Worthington once told her that his wife disobeyed his (Worthington's) priesthood authority as family patriarch by having the surgery.

In their book, *The God Makers*, Ed Decker and Dave Hunt, said, "Something radical and hard to describe takes place in one's self-image when he believes he is destined to become a god and rule over an entire universe…" (pg. 50) "Grasping after godhood breeds pride and arrogance, and warps one's thinking in a multitude of subtle ways." (pg. 52)

Certainly one could say that Worthington was warped in a major way. His wife divorced him, and he was transferred to a prison in Nevada, where he committed suicide a year later. He died a lonely, broken man without hope of ever becoming the god he so desperately tried to become.

In a society where having one or two children is the norm, and birth control is almost universally accepted, even by many Catholics, actions such as Worthington's must seem totally irrational. Given my experience with the mindset of Mormon males reared in a Utah patriarchal society, however, it makes perfectly good sense to me. Numbers of children are crucial. All too often the "number" one has far outweighs any considerations of financial circumstance or the physical abilities of the mother to care for them. Publicly, church leaders state that, although financial circumstances are not a valid consideration for preventing pregnancy, the woman's physical health ought to be considered.

All too often that is not the case. Women end up bearing a tremendous burden in their quest to be obedient to their husbands and help them obtain the Celestial Kingdom in the next life. Although few will openly admit their concerns, for fear of reprisals from church authorities, I've seen the aftermath of the countless pregnancies, miscarriages, and numerous children born in too rapid a succession to be healthy for the woman.

It spite of the rhetoric about women holding a high place alongside God in the creation of human beings, the male priesthood that holds itself in much higher esteem more often overlooks women.

6

༁༃

Mormon Women in Utah: Osmond Family Syndrome

*L*earning to cope with rearing a large family requires much patience, stamina, and creativity on the part of women. I had one friend who had nine children, and the oldest was only fifteen! "How do you manage to get everyone dressed for church on time?" I asked her one day.

"It's pretty much every kid for himself," she replied. "If someone can't find his shoes, he goes to church in his sock feet."

In most families, the oldest children help the younger ones, and it becomes a cooperative effort to get ready for anything. I often noticed how little the men seemed to be involved in the family life. Except for being around for Family Home Evening on Monday night (the one night of the week the church sets aside for family activities) and on Sunday, most of the men I knew were remote toward their families. Of course, most worked long hours just to make enough money to support such large broods. With the church's negative attitude toward working women, it fell to the men to make the entire living, a difficult task given the dramatic economic inflation of the 1970s. But the men seemed remote in other ways also. Many appeared to me to be distant emotionally. Perhaps is was the strain of having responsibility for such a large family and the concern about money.

A large family places financial hardship on average, middle-class people. Lack of money often took its toll on the marriages I observed in Utah. But Mormons know how to be thrifty and work hard at making everything stretch. Most families had a garden of some kind in which food was grown and preserved to help with the tremendous food bills a large family can incur. Utah is probably the "Casserole Capital" of the world. Relief Society "homemaking" meetings were often dedicated to 101 ways to prepare a pound of hamburger to feed a small army. If hamburger was too gourmet, there was always soy-substitute. Bought in bulk, it was a fraction of the price of hamburger. With spices, a lot of tomato sauce, onions, green peppers, and some imagination, it could be made to taste just like hamburger.

I learned to be just as thrifty as the next Mormon. Dee and I had a house on a half-acre lot with seventeen fruit trees and a quarter-acre garden plot. Having been raised on a farm, I loved the land. Digging in the soil was one of my favorite things to do, and it was far from being work. I soon became an excellent gardener, and every summer I spent long, hard hours gardening and canning enough fruits and vegetables to see us through to the next growing season. Averaging about five hundred quarts of everything from peaches, applesauce, bing cherries, and pears to green beans, pickled beets, tomatoes, and tomato sauce to jellies and jams of all types, I was able to feed a family of six on about one hundred dollars a month throughout the 1970s. I made or baked just about everything we ate from scratch including cakes, pies, bread, pancakes, and waffles. In the winter, after gardening was done, I sewed clothes for the kids and myself.

Oddly enough, I achieved a level of contentedness during those years that I had never known before. I took great pride in my homemaking accomplishments. In addition to winning acceptance in the Mormon community and among my female peers, I began accepting myself. I had never before felt as contented as after we became part of the community of Kaysville Mormonism. In Kaysville, Utah, within the heart of Mormonism, I found not only a place in which to be accepted but a way to achieve that acceptance. And I could do it without denying my basic nature—creativity. All the gardening, canning, cooking, and preparing satisfied that urge in me to be doing something that reflected my creativity. Although writing was my first love, as it had been since early childhood, I never felt confident enough to try to be a writer. So, I settled for doing creative things that all good Mormon wives and mothers do. Those first few years in Kaysville, when I closed my eyes to the outside world and immersed myself in the warmth and goodness of what I believed was the perfect religion in the perfect society, were the happiest times of my life. At one point, I would have been content to freeze those years in time and never move on to anything different.

Yet, while I was feeling so content on the one hand, I was also learning much about the facade that Mormons erect around their lives, particularly the women. As with anything that seems perfect, too good to be true, there is bound to be a fatal flaw. Everyone was too smiling, too happy, afflicted with something I would eventually come to call the "Osmond Family Syndrome."

ജ

The subtle pressure placed on Mormons by church leaders to be the perfect people that the church "sells" to the world, to present the perpetual happy face, creates problems for those who discover that the ideals of the church do not always match up to the realities of life. The church television commercials that depict large, happy, smiling families, full of love, as the norm for Mormon society fail to tell the whole story. Although as in every segment of society, there are happy people, the cloak of idealism placed around Mormons as a people is pure public relations. Several years ago as part of the church's advertising campaign, it placed a removable insert in the *Reader's Digest* called "Seven Keys to Mormonism." The twelve-page booklet was an attempt to clear up many misconceptions that people might have about the Mormon Church. It offered free booklets, which could be ordered from the church.

The first section of the booklet, titled "Home and Family Come First" pointed out how close-knit and happy all Mormon families are. It stated that although there are many threats to the American home and family life, "most Mormon homes, because of their religious convictions, are as secure now as they were in pioneer days. In the typical Mormon home today you'll find a generously larger than average family—four to six children, or even more. It will be a family likely to be admired by neighbors for its quiet competence and self-assurance, and generally envied for its closeness and good-natured round of shared activities." This is the Osmond Family Syndrome epitomized.

In section two, "Try Always to Stand on Your Own Feet," it says that Mormons "believe that it's wrong to ask anyone else to help them in time of difficulty until they and their family have exhausted every personal resource at their command." This section gave the reader the correct impression that Mormons are extremely self-reliant. It also gave the incorrect impression that good Mormons are very prosperous. "Most Mormon families live comfortably in homes they own or are buying." The pamphlet never said anything about the families I saw struggling just to pay the rent, never mind saving enough to purchase a house. In section three, "Work is Something to Enjoy," it stated that Mormons are hard workers—which they are. "Most of us with time to spare will relax; most Mormons will look for more work to do," said the booklet. However, you know what they say about all work and no play. In a "pressure-cooker society" (as one Utah psychologist I know calls it) such as Utah, where learning to relax could greatly benefit the general population, Mormons have a way of making people feel guilty if they are not working eighteen hours a day. I saw friends work to point of near exhaustion. Later I would do the same, yet still feel guilty about taking time out to do something for myself. In this section it mentioned by name the Osmond family as a good example of a family that works all the time.

Section five talked about the good health that Mormons enjoy due to temperate living and keeping the Word of Wisdom, which brings not only good physical health but good mental health. "Good health, clean living—it shows, in Mormons. It shows in their clear, friendly gaze. Nothing to hide. Nothing nagging at their conscience. . . Doctors attribute [longevity] to the Word of Wisdom. To that, and to spiritual poise, lack of mental and emotional stress. Mormons say, 'We're just high on life—that's all.'"

When I remember the many problems that I encountered in Utah, problems generated by living in a society that encouraged perfection as the standard—which generates tremendous emotional and mental stress—I become angry at the Mormon Church's attempt to pass its standards off as the ideal to which every family in the world should attain. The idea that Mormons have no stress in their lives and that they have neither mental problems nor hidden problems just is not true.

I knew so many in that society who lived the split consciousness and suffered terribly for it. I knew women who went to Salt
Lake City to see psychologists, hoping that no one would find
out they needed help coping with their lives. To them, hiding
the stress, the unhappiness that is normal at some point in all of
our lives, was mandatory. Keeping the church's image of the
happy family alive and well was of overwhelming importance;
and there is another reason for this attitude.

As a religion, Mormonism teaches that if one is living by all
the rules and regulations of the church and in complete obedience
to the Prophet, who is the head of the church, one is happy.
Church leaders would have the world believe that life is just that
simple. On the surface, the early impression I received in my Mormon journey, was that problems that afflict others do not afflict
faithful Mormons. If you have problems, then you must not be
living in complete accord with all the laws of Mormonism. This
"I am a Mormon, therefore I am happy" syndrome is all pervasive
in Utah Mormon society. If you have problems, or if you are unhappy, you never, never let anyone on the outside know about it.
It is not only bad for public relations, but it can be unhealthy for
the individual. I know of a case where a woman went to her bishop
for help and suddenly found herself facing ridicule and church dis-
cipline instead of receiving the help she so desperately needed.

Therein lies one of the basic problems. Mormons are encouraged to consult the ward bishop as their first line of assis-
tance. If necessary, he will direct you to a Mormon psychologist
or psychiatrist, so that your problems can be kept within the
"family." That's why the Mormon Church has a closet full of
skeletons and why members are encouraged to keep the doors
shut on their own skeletons as well. No one must know that anyone within the hallowed walls of Mormonism is unhappy or
troubled—especially those outside the church whom the
church tries so hard to convert.

The problems that plague society as a whole have not bypassed Utah, despite the church's attempt to sweep them under the rug. Spousal (primarily wife) abuse, childhood sexual abuse, and drug and alcohol abuse are all part the fabric of Utah. Because of the high population of Mormons—both good Mormons and jack-Mormons—society's problems affect them, whether they like to admit it or not. To what degree is unclear. Accurate statistics are difficult to obtain, because of the priesthood network that keeps most of these crimes in the "family."

Unfortunately, the perpetrators of such crimes as sexual abuse, child molestation, and wife beating often go unpunished by either the secular legal system (because the crime is never reported) or by the church (because the church keeps silent or tells the abuser to repent, and go and sin no more). Other states have taken measures directly aimed at the Mormon Church to make it a felony to conceal the confession of a crime. In 1996 the Arizona Court of Appeals ordered three Mormon bishops to reveal confessions from a former church member convicted of child molestation. These three men had refused to answer questions under oath in a lawsuit filed by the mother of a two-year-old child who was molested while under the care of a man who was then a member of the Mormon Church in Arizona. The mother, Cynthia Brown, accused officers of the church of negligence in their attempts to counsel Kenneth Ray when he admitted to them nearly twenty years ago that he had a "sexual problem." According to an article that appeared in the *Phoenix Gazette*, Ray gave up his clergy-penitent privilege when he confessed to the crimes, and his confessors were left with no independent right to invoke the privilege, said an appeals court judge.

In 1990, an Arizona woman actually brought suit against the Mormon Church after a branch president[26] and a bishop encouraged her to entrust her three sons to the custody of her ex-husband, who had only recently been released from prison after being convicted of child molestation. The woman had to be hospitalized for an extended period due to a brain tumor, and the church officials assured her that they would watch closely over her sons. They told her that her former husband would in no way be involved with the scouting program, in which her sons were involved. The suit claimed her ex-husband was not only allowed to serve in the church as assistant scoutmaster, but that their father again molested her sons. I was not able to obtain information on how this was settled, but the typical pattern would have been for the church to quietly settle it.

With recent revelations concerning the number of pedophiles that have served and continue to serve in leadership capacities in the Boy Scouts of America, one has to wonder what numbers are serving in the Mormon Church in the same capacity. The scouting program is one of the largest ongoing activities in the Mormon Church, and it would be ludicrous to believe that this problem, which has tainted scouting nationwide, has not also touched the huge program in Utah and the Mormon Church specifically.

Part of the reason for inept counseling at the level of bishop is the fact that laymen hold these high positions of authority. As much as I agree with the idea of lay volunteers in principle, using lay people as bishops has inherent dangers. Many people go to their bishops, just as Protestants go to their ministers, to request help with personal problems, many of them severe in nature,

---

26   A branch is similar to a ward, but much smaller, and is usually found in sparsely populated rural areas or areas where the church has few members. The branch president is the presiding authority.

such as the above-mentioned child molester. These men who serve as the spiritual leaders of wards are plumbers, electricians, school teachers, salesmen, and factory workers who have absolutely no training whatsoever in counseling or psychology. The best advice they can offer is often nothing more than Mormon rhetoric—"It's against Heavenly Father's laws," "repent," "when you feel the urge to do this, pray or begin singing a church hymn in your head." These remedies are hardly enough for someone with a serious problem such as pedophilia. Only recently, due in part to lawsuits, has the church counseled its bishops to advise people with serious mental or emotional problems to seek professional help. How many actually do however, is unknown. The repercussions of bad advice are often far reaching.

Recently a young woman employed with a small company that a friend of mine and his wife (both non-Mormons) own, was brutally beaten by her priesthood-holding husband. When she came into work one morning terribly battered, my friend urged her to call the police and report it. Although she was reluctant at first ("Everyone will know we're not the perfect family!"), she finally allowed my friend to call for help. She filled out the paper work and pressed charges. What she didn't count on however, was a visit that evening from the bishop of her ward who "counseled" her to drop the charges against her husband and get him out of jail. After all, he was an Elder in the church, a priesthood holder. She shouldn't jeopardize her eternal life, he told her, by turning on her husband at a time when she should stand by him and help him with his problem. The next day she told my friend what the bishop had said, called the police, and dropped the charges. Two days later, upon her bishop's advice, she told my friend, "I'm being given bad advice by people who don't know what the church is really all about, so I can't stay on with you." Like many Mormon women, she was accustomed to doing what men told her; she quit her job, as her bishop had advised her to do.

Another example involved my friend, Karen, who lived nearby. Her little girl, who was about seven at the time, and my daughter, who was the same age, used to play at each other's homes. Unbeknownst to anyone in the neighborhood, Karen's husband was molesting their children. When she found out he was molesting their daughter, she went to the bishop. The bishop counseled with them. The husband apologized and promised he would not do it again.

Not long afterward, Karen took her five-year-old son to the doctor to see why he was having constant bouts of diarrhea, problems controlling his bowels, and was messing himself. The doctor gave her the shocking news. The boy was being subjected to anal intercourse by an adult male. Karen knew it was her husband. This time she called the sheriff, filed charges against her husband, and got a court order to keep him away from the children, despite church "counsel" that she not deprive him of his "patriarchal" rights to see his children. She took action against the continuing advice of our bishop not to resort to legal recourse against her husband. However, it was only after she took advantage of the legal system, that the neighborhood found out about this man's crimes against his children. It frightened us to think what might have happened to our own children had this man been allowed to continue his behavior unchecked or untreated by professionals. That a legalistic religion like Mormonism can produce what Sonia Johnson calls "sexual cripples" is very evident in Utah Mormon society.

While I assumed for the better part of the ten years I spent in Kaysville that most of my Mormon friends were happy in their "calling" as wives and mothers and had perfect families, I began to see through the facades, the pretenses that many of them lived. Until that realization, I was happy. Life was simple with all the rules outlined, and if I stayed within the lines, nothing would be too complicated. I bought into it all, as I too became the perfect wife and mother—the perfect Mormon convert.

7
ೞೞ

Mormon Women in Utah: Behind the Shroud

Mormon theology is the most denigrating to the women of the church whose position of subservience to and total dependence on their husbands financially, emotionally, and spiritually often puts them in a position of never being allowed to speak out, or at the least forcing them to take care in what they say. However, the men also suffer under the strain of a theology that places undue burdens on them. Without a faithful, priesthood-holding husband to call her forth on the day of resurrection, a Mormon woman cannot go to the highest degree of "glory." If this had seemed a beautiful idea to me at first, it did not take me long to discover the tragedy in this theology and the absolute power it gives men over their wives.

In addition, men hold the unenviable position of being responsible for the salvation of their wives. After living in

Mormonism's heart for several years I came to understand the destructive nature of this belief not only to the women, but also to the men who have tremendous pressures placed on them as well. I did not learn this aspect of Mormon theology until very late in my Mormon experience. Had I known sooner, I might have left the church earlier. (Mormon missionaries are careful not to teach the deeper or more controversial theologies of the church during the time they are giving lessons to new, potential converts. They are taught to stick to the basics, win the converts, then let them discover these other issues of doctrine later when they are too deeply entrenched in the religion to extract themselves easily.) On the other hand, perhaps I would have overlooked this as I did so many of the doctrinal points with which I disagreed.

Bruce R. McConkie, long considered one of the greatest authorities on Mormon doctrine, said, "Husbands must . . . love their wives, sacrifice for their well-being and salvation, and guide them in holiness until they are cleansed, sanctified, and perfected, until they are prepared for exaltation in that glorious heaven where the family unit continues. Husbands thus become the saviors of their wives." (Doctrinal New Testament Commentary, 2:519)

When, I found the above quote in my husband's priesthood study lesson manual, which the men use in their Sunday priesthood meetings, I was appalled. All my life, my Christian upbringing had emphasized that, for Christians, Jesus Christ is the Savior. HE and HE alone can cleanse us of our sins and through HIS grace bring us to sanctification and ultimately perfection. What McConkie was saying is that mere mortal men have the horrible and awesome burden of cleansing their obviously unclean wives, of perfecting them in spite of the fact that men are no more perfect than the women they are supposedly preparing for exaltation! Talk about pressure!

However, it is not only men that teach that they are on a much higher plain than women are. Other women betray their sex by teaching that without a man, a woman is nothing. Elaine Cannon, a woman who served in the church in several executive capacities during the years I was a member, in an address at Brigham Young University on February 10, 1970, said to the students: "What would we do without the priesthood? We need you men. We need you to counsel with the Lord, that you may guide us, set us straight, and then we will salute you and do your bidding." That blatant promotion of absolute submissiveness to male authority, both to husband and church, represses Mormon women and keeps them where the church wants them: at home pregnant, raising good Mormon children. It implies that women are not capable of going to the Lord on their own to receive counseling, that somehow receiving their own direction from God is off limits to women.

Yet the church claims that being a wife and mother are the highest callings to which a woman can aspire. The church places women on pedestals, extolling the virtues of their role in helping their husbands achieve godhood. Sonia Johnson claims in her book, *Housewife to Heretic,* that all this rhetoric by the priesthood is "a deliberate attempt to distract women from noticing what is really happening to them in their lives." It was in getting to know these women of Kaysville, who became my friends, loved me, and trusted me with their innermost thoughts and fears, that I came to understand Mormonism's deepest fallacies.

Looking at their lives as one looks in through a window from the outside—for even though deeply entrenched in Mormonism, in a certain way I would always be an outsider, a stranger in Zion—I learned just how terribly damaging a legalistic, patriarchal religion can be to its men and women.

Ron Carlson, short story author, Mormon, and writing professor at Arizona State University, once commented, "The first thing any religion worth its salt controls is its women . . ." The church controls the men, then leaves it to the men to control the women.

Mormon women are taught submission to male priesthood authority from early childhood. Love for one's husband and submission to this male authority are synonymous. In an article titled "The Way To Christlike Love," appearing in the December 1982 issue of the church's *Ensign* magazine, Allen E. Bergin states, "A woman need have no fear of being imposed upon or of any dictatorial measures or any improper demands when the husband is self-sacrificing and worthy. Certainly no intelligent woman would hesitate to give submission to her own truly righteous husband in everything. We are sometimes shocked to see the wife take over the leadership, naming the one to pray, the place to be, the thing to do." Notice the way Bergin said that no "intelligent" woman would hesitate to submit, thus linking this highly valued Mormon ideal—intelligence—with submission. Yet in the next statement, he encourages women not to think by saying that the man should make all the decisions. Is it any wonder that Utah Mormon women are so intellectually shackled and emotionally impaired? Is it any wonder that, in their own minds, the men become superior beings with all power and authority to do anything to their wives and children that they deem in their best interest?

In fact, the attitude toward Utah Mormon women is not much different than it is toward Muslim fundamentalist women in the Middle Ease who must keep their heads covered in public, never drive a car, never talk to a man who is not her husband, and never allow her photograph to be taken. Although the signs are not so outwardly apparent, Utah Mormon women are just as shackled by church patriarchy as are Muslim women. From early childhood, Mormon girls are taught that their highest and best "calling" in life is that of wife and mother. To bring

children into the world—providing physical bodies for the multitudes of spirits that awaits such vehicles—and to nurture those
beings is a woman's sole purpose. In her book, *Housewife to Heretic*, Sonia Johnson said, "The message from society—doubly
underlined by the church—that since I was female I was only
suited for wife and motherhood."

Marriage to a worthy priesthood holder becomes the ultimate goal for young girls, so that by the time a girl graduates
from high school, marriage is not just a goal, but an obsession.
In 1980, statistics showed that seventy-five percent of Utah's
brides were teen-agers. That trend continues today, although
the percentage is down somewhat to seventy percent.

Too often, the pressure brought to bear on young people to
marry—and marry right, i.e., in the temple—is so great they
jump into marriage with the first person that comes along. Many
of the young girls I knew found a boyfriend in high school,
waited until he returned from his mission, and immediately
jumped into marriage (as young returned missionaries are encouraged by the church to do). The result was often a relationship whose real meaning was distorted by a long separation and
the heightened sex drive of these young people.

A letter to Dr. Brent Barlow, who wrote a marriage and family advice column for the *Deseret News* during the time I lived in
Utah, said, "My wife and I have been married for almost a year
now and keep waiting for something to happen. But it never
does. Where is all the ecstatic joy and fulfillment that is supposed to come with marriage? Have we missed something along
the way or are we unrealistic in our expectations?" The doctor
explained that marriage is "like a garden: you can't just wait for
something to happen, you must plant seeds, cultivate and care
for the garden before something happens." (Mormons understand gardening.)

The pressure just to be married—to anyone—was so great that good Mormons often leapt into matrimony solely for the sake of being married, without the experience of dating a variety of people and waiting for the right one. In addition, the church paints such an idealistic picture of marriage, that often when the realities of life set in, great disappointment results. The pressure to be married can lead to marriages lacking in real passion and love.

Many of my friends lived in what I perceived as loveless marriages. For them, happiness seemed to be an elusive goal pushed out of reach by marrying too quickly, too young. Constant pressure from church leaders to marry exacerbated the problem. They preached that marriage was the ultimate ideal to which men and women could attain, that marriage produced the ultimate in happiness and fulfillment for everyone who entered into the union. There was no excuse for anyone not marrying, except for mental or physical disabilities that would make marriage impossible.

€€€

∽⃝⃝

If marriage was the ideal, divorce was out of the question. Divorce in Kaysville was rare. When there was a divorce, we would shake our heads in sadness at the misguided ways of poor Sister So-and-so who forsook all—even her eternal life—and for what? Over the years, of all the people I knew in town, I can think of only two who divorced. The community completely understood the woman who divorced her husband because he sexually molested their children.

The other woman asked her husband for a divorce. We never knew why, and no one ever asked her. Her children were almost grown, and she was the typical Mormon housewife and mother. When word raced through the ward like a Kansas prairie fire that Francis had asked Tom for a divorce, there was more than mere shock at the impropriety of the action. The women were amazed that Francis would sacrifice everything—even her eternal life—for that alien world of singleness. We wondered what sort of sad, unfulfilled life Francis would lead without a priesthood leader in her life, not by chance of death or accident, but by deliberate choice. It was a choice none of us could fathom, and it never occurred to us that she could be happier without him than with him.

The church, which tends to promote the "idealistics" of life, rather than the reality, does not consider that marriage may not be for everyone, or that a person can—under pressure to choose someone, anyone—choose the wrong person. Sometimes, no matter how much you cultivate, if the soil is dead, nothing will grow. For a member to remain single is not an option in the eyes of church officials, who continue to pressure people into marriage. For those who do not marry, the pressure is even greater.

I was amazed by this seemingly nineteenth-century thinking in the latter part of the twentieth. Young women are generally married by age twenty or twenty-one, and a woman still single at the age of twenty-four or twenty-five is considered the next thing to an Old Maid. A dear friend and neighbor had four daughters, all of whom married as they were supposed to except the youngest. Cari went to college and obtained a degree, then served an eighteen-month mission for the church. After returning, she began working in Salt Lake City. She eventually returned to college for a graduate degree and bought a comfortable home. As far as I can tell from communication with her mother, Cari is quite happy.

Because so few Mormon girls exercise their option not to marry, Cari was viewed almost as a freak. Cari's singleness does not seem to bother her mother, but it sure bothers other people who keep asking her mother when Cari is going to get married. "I wish people would quit asking me that," Cari's mother told me one day. "It's nobody's business whether she's married or not."

The pressures Cari and other women like her (what few there are) face are overwhelming in a society where a woman's life is validated almost entirely through her husband and the number of children she has. It is unthinkable in the minds of most Mormons that a woman of marriageable age would choose to remain single, and actually be happy with the choice. In fact, it took the church years to recognize the fact that there was a growing single population within its ranks whose needs should be addressed in other ways than just by putting more pressure on them to marry.

In 1984, an Associated Press article that said that a governor's task force on women reported that "traditional Utah attitudes that encourage women to marry early and stay at home with their families are causing poverty, despair and guilt among women, and should be changed." The report went on to say that, "The belief that a woman's place is in the home, rooted in the family-centered teachings of the predominant Mormon Church, leave[s] women ill-equipped to deal with divorce or the death of a husband."

Contributing to this difficult situation is the fact that while education for both males and females is greatly encouraged by the church, fewer females than males actually finish their college education. Because so many girls go to college merely to pass the time until their missionary boyfriends come home to marry them, or to find a suitable Mormon boy to marry, often they find themselves (as Jeff and Sue did, in the previous chapter) with a baby on the way so that she must curtail her education.

I knew very few young girls from Kaysville who were attending college with any serious thoughts of a career. The church is not shy about letting young women know that their place is in the home rearing a large family and that putting a career ahead of that is frowned upon. A woman's college education, if she obtains one, should be used for the betterment of the home, family, and church over and above the promotion of a career. I heard this philosophy preached many times during my life as a Mormon.

I can hardly speak of the pressures to marry that the church brings to bear on its females without also mentioning that same pressure is exerted on its male priesthood holders. The church frowns on the idea of young men waiting until age twenty-three or twenty-four to marry. It encourages marriage as soon as young members "marriageable age," which for the men means as soon as they return from their missions.

Frank M. returned from his mission and still did not have a girlfriend. For two years after his return, he worked and attended school, but kept himself unattached. Everyone in Kaysville was trying to get Frank "fixed up" with one of the eligible young girls in the community. At one of the semiannual, church-wide priesthood meetings held in Salt Lake City, the emphasis was on finding a mate and marrying. Church leaders had heard that young people were putting off marriage until they finished school and other such "nonsense." Church authorities admonished the men that if they were of marriageable age (twenty or twenty-one by Mormon standards) and not yet married, they were committing a grave error and should seek to marry as soon as possible in order to fulfill their priesthood calling.

After Frank returned from this meeting, feeling guilty about his single status, he married the first girl he dated, according to his mother, who had some reservations about the relationship. The marriage was not a good one from the start. His mother often lamented to me that he married too quickly, under pressure from the church. I do not know whether the marriage ended in divorce or not.

ಐಐಡ

Young Mormons in Utah not only feel the pressure to marry early, but tremendous pressure is placed on them to marry in the temple, and often with disastrous consequences. Since the only true marriage in the Mormon Church is one that takes place in one of the many temples scattered throughout the world, good Mormon families feel a great stigma placed upon them if their children do not marry in the temple. Mormon parents often go to great lengths to see to it that their children marry in the temple, sometimes regardless of the young peoples' "spiritual" status. One of my best friends is now a jack Mormon, but was a good Mormon girl during her youth, despite her penchant for going astray and questioning church authority. At eighteen, Margie found herself pregnant by a recently returned—and obviously very "horny" (as Margie likes to say)—missionary. Their parents were appalled, but knew it was absolutely mandatory that the couple marry in the temple (more to preserve their good standing in the church and community than out of any consideration for Margie and her boyfriend). Many times in Utah it is not what you know or how you behave, it is who you know and how high up you are on the church ladder that allows a person to accomplish things that would otherwise be impossible.

Margie's parents were longtime Mormons from good "pioneer" stock, and her father was quite high up in the stake hierarchy at that time. Margie's husband-to-be had parents in a similar position. Between the two sets of parents, they managed to get the couple a temple recommend. They hurried the pair through a ceremony, complete with white temple clothing. Many years later, after I had become friends with Margie, who was then in her mid-forties, she told me that she had not even wanted to marry the guy. She said that the whole temple marriage thing had been a farce from the beginning, but that they'd cooperated with their parents to help them save face in the community. Margie was in her mid-thirties when she divorced her husband after having four children with him. Margie is the only jack Mormon in her family, the "black sheep" and virtually outcast among her brothers and sisters, who are all active Mormons and hold high positions within various church organizations.

Recently, Margie's daughter, who was forty-two and newly divorced from her husband after twenty years of marriage and four children, remarried in the temple. Her new husband, a man ten years her junior, who was also divorced and had two young children. To pull off a temple marriage, Margie's daughter had to first get church authorities to give her a temple divorce from her first husband (usually a difficult, time-consuming process). After that was quickly accomplished, the couple had to obtain a temple recommend. The two had been seeing each other and sleeping together for almost a year. Margie did not know if her daughter was attending church or tithing, nor did she know whether the young man was either. Still, they obtained a recommend, because his parents knew the right people and pulled the right strings to have the marriage done properly. Margie laughed when she related this to me. "It's all still as much as farce today as it was when I was eighteen," she said.

꿍ᘓ

In most Christian denominations, many more women than men are religious and actively participating in the life of the church. Although Mormonism has a high degree of participation by its male members, it is typical to see a greater number of women actively involved in the church than men. I knew many women who attended church alone because their husbands were jack Mormons who were not active for one reason or another. Most of the men that I knew personally who were jack-

Mormons were not active because they did not keep the Word of Wisdom. These women were brave to participate in the life of the Mormon Church without their husbands, because in Mormonism, as in no other religion, the prevalent thinking is that "I am nothing without a man."

Although women who are not married in the temple and whose husbands do not participate with them at church are not intentionally made to feel on the fringes, most of those I knew in this situation felt as if they lived on the periphery of Mormonism. Mormon doctrine, which is patriarchal in content, contributes to women's feelings of inadequacy, low self-esteem, and worthlessness if they are not married in the temple to an active priesthood holder. It did not take me long to discover that without temple marriage I would never be completely a part of Mormonism. I am sure that the women who had grown up in the Utah church must have understood this since they were teenagers.

However, there is no accounting for love. For those who fall in love and marry jack-Mormons or non-Mormons, life in the church is full, if not complete. Sandra was a very committed Mormon woman, married to a wonderful man with whom she had had only two children (she said because of birth complications). She was a good worker in the ward, seemingly happy and always laughing and smiling. I came to know and love her during my years there. However, under her happiness lay the pall that she had not yet been married in the temple, something she had grown to desire more than anything in the world.

As Sandra grew older, she began to think more about life after death. She was worried about the prospects of never seeing her husband, whom she loved dearly, again in the next life. Even worse were thoughts of being given to another man, with whom she would have to spend eternity, because her own husband had not achieved the Celestial Kingdom. I don't know whether Sandra ever achieved her goal, but when I left Utah, she was still working diligently on her husband to make him "worthy" to qualify for a temple recommend so they could be sealed for eternity. (He smoked and drank beer, so she was trying to get him to stop those two habits.) I sincerely hope it worked for her. For some men, the pressure to be an active part of Mormonism becomes too much.

The pressure many women place on their husbands to participate in the life of the church and become worthy for temple marriage often causes severe rifts in the marriage, or even divorce. Another woman, Patricia, had the most handsome husband anyone could ever want. He was a successful businessman, and together they had four of the most beautiful children I had ever seen. The couple met when she was only nineteen, at a dance at Hill Air Force Base, north of Kaysville in Clearfield, Utah. He was a tall, dashing uniformed officer, and she fell head over heels in love with him on the spot. The only problem was that he was a Catholic. He knew nothing about Mormonism and she knew nothing about Catholicism, but chemistry knows no religious bounds. They fell in love and married.

As she told me years later, when you are nineteen and eager for marriage, and your Prince Charming rides right up and sweeps you off your feet, religious compatibility is the last thing on your mind. Besides, "marry them now, convert them later" was the usual line of thinking. So they married in a religiously neutral setting and began their life together.

After he left the Air Force, they moved back to the East Coast, where they raised their children. It was not a problem for him that she wanted to raise their children Mormon, so long as they could be taught something of the Catholic faith, which would enable them to choose for themselves which religion they preferred when they were older. However, the children adhered to their mother's Mormonism throughout their teenage years.

During this time, Patricia became increasingly desperate to have a temple marriage, to seal their lives and their family for time and all eternity. What she did not realize was that she had met her match in her Catholic husband. If there is one religious group of people that is as convinced that it is God's true church as Mormons are, it is Catholics. Theologically, these two religions run quite parallel, which is why many Catholics convert easily to Mormonism. However, this was not to be the case with Patricia and her husband.

In spite of the fact that she left Mormon literature laying all over the house, so that her husband would pick it up and read it, and despite her having missionaries over for dinner frequently so they could talk to him, he refused to join the Mormon Church. She became increasingly obsessed with getting him to the temple, so much so that she spent most of their time together begging him to join the church so they could spend eternity together. They were such a perfect family, she reasoned, why only have it for this life? Why could they not have it for always? After nearly twenty-five years of marriage, the rift Patricia created in her marriage with her incessant pleading, grew to a chasm. One day, her husband came home and announced he was leaving her and would be seeking a divorce. Her fairy tale marriage to her Prince Charming was over, ruined by her obsessive desire for temple marriage.

Patricia moved with her youngest child, who was by that time a teenager, back to Utah, where she immediately began her search for a man to take her to the temple. Within a year, she had found him, and they were married in the temple. Although she was not married to the man of her dreams, she was at least assured of salvation and the eternal "good life" in the Celestial Kingdom. I often wonder if Patricia has achieved true happiness.

Many Mormon temple marriages endure a lifetime not because of love or commitment, but because church officials are reluctant to advise divorce under any circumstance. If there are pressures to marry, there are equal pressures to remain married, regardless of the circumstance. For example, there was a beautiful woman named Anna, whom I came to love and admire very much. A strong, intelligent woman, she was married at a very young age to a young military officer. After his career with the military ended, they settled in Kaysville to raise their family. When I first knew Anna, her children were mostly grown, except for a son about fourteen or fifteen. She lived in a beautiful, large house and drove the newest luxury car. Everything seemed wonderful on the surface, but as we grew closer—drawn together by our love of drama—I began to see that her life was far from the fairy tale existence that it appeared on the surface to be.

I learned that her husband and she had not shared a bed in many years. Due to a business he owned, he was a very wealthy man. He kept Anna well with a nice weekly allowance, the new car, and anything else she wanted—that money could buy. But he was seldom around. In fact, during all the years we were friends, I only saw her husband once. He kept a mistress in an apartment somewhere in Salt Lake City and spent much of his time there, coming to see Anna infrequently. Anna's face, with its delicate, finely chiseled features, was a perpetual mask of pain and humiliation. Her laughter, during our mutual activities in the community, seemed to reflect some inner strength she had found to endure a loveless marriage to an absentee husband.

One day I asked why she just did not get a divorce and try to find happiness with someone else before it was too late.

"I have a very good friend who's close to the General Authorities," she said. "I went to him one day and told him about Howard and his mistress. I told him I wanted both a civil and temple divorce from Howard. But, he advised me to stay in the marriage. He said that Howard would be mine in the next life, and ending our marriage at this time in our lives isn't advisable. Besides, what if I don't find another man to take me to the temple? All this will have been for nothing."

Looking at Anna, I could not imagine staying in a loveless marriage and enduring unhappiness in this life, even if it meant going to hell in the next, if one believes in such a place. (Hell for Mormons means being in absolute darkness without one's family.) It would have never occurred to Anna to go against the advice she received and divorce her husband. Good Mormon women rarely exercise their individuality by thinking independently of the church's leaders. (Of course, there was never any mention that Howard might not make it to the Celestial Kingdom due to his infidelity and adulterous relationship with a mistress! Mormon men stick together.)

The more I read about and studied Mormonism, the more my friends and acquaintances began telling me their problems—most of which centered around husbands who were already practicing to be "God" by exercising their high and mighty authority over their wives and making them feel inferior—the angrier I got. Having been raised a Christian, I knew that I, as a woman, was loved and accepted by God just as I was. I could do my own praying and receive my own counsel from the Lord. I did not need a man to intercede for me. And I certainly did not need one to be my savior!

That the church uses its priesthood power and organizations such as Relief Society to keep blinders on its women is an insult to women's intelligence. But most of my Mormon friends just accepted their role and did not question the narrowness of their lives. Perhaps that is why, after I began working, I was drawn to people I met at work whom were non-Mormons and jack Mormons. I found them to have so much more depth and to be so much more interesting than my friends and acquaintances in Kaysville.

I often marveled at how quickly female conversation waned when the topic turned to anything beyond home, family, and church. For most of my female friends, there was nothing beyond those basic concerns that was deemed worthy of their attention. Most had not gone to college, very few had ever held a job of any kind, much less had a career, and almost none of my friends had any ambitions beyond being a wife and mother. All their lives they had been taught that to want anything outside home and family was wrong. They lived lives of quiet humility and submission to priesthood authority, wanting little for themselves, expecting even less. They were told repeatedly that they were completely fulfilled in their roles as wife and mother. For the most part, they believed it.

In my own life, it became a struggle to continue to believe in and accept Mormonism due to the points of doctrine that I felt were contrary to the Christian teachings I had learned during my youth. There were days when I felt the nudge of some unseen hand and the whisper of an unknown voice urging me beyond the comfort zone I had reached as a good Mormon housewife and mother. If being those things was the ultimate calling for my friends, I knew from somewhere deep in my soul, that it was not mine. However, for several years I was able to brush away the hand and ignore the voice, as I became very much a part of the community. I considered leaving the church at one point, about six years into my journey, but decided that I could do more good by staying within the walls of Mormonism and helping other women whenever I could. Although it was a big task, I believed that these women in Kaysville somehow needed me.

8

ଚ୍ଚ

Mormon Men in Utah: The Savior Role

The attitude of the majority of Mormon men I knew was one that baffled me at first, but the deeper I delved into Mormon theology, the more I came to realize they took the godhood thing very seriously. Many lorded over their wives and children as if they owned them, and in a way they did, having been given permission by the church to rule over their families. I found this attitude intimidating for several years, then finally just downright disgusting. My own husband was a kind, passive-natured man who treated me equally, as a partner. Besides, he hardly had a choice. Being the dominant one in the relationship, I was the decision maker; the one that when action was called for, I took action.

It was just my "first-born" nature to grab the bull by the horns and handle things. It was his nature to let me handle things on the home front, while he ran a business we owned at Salt Lake City International Airport. Our relationship was surprising to my female friends who did not understand my aggressive way of getting things done, and I'm sure Dee's male priesthood-holder friends thought he was allowing me too much authority in the home. We were very much the opposite of typical male-female relationship, which I observed among my Mormon friends. Actually, I think he lacked the ambition to become a god and the interest. He certainly lacked the tremendous ego that it requires for a man to believe that he can be a god.

It did not go unobserved however, that contrary to Mormon doctrine, Dee was not the absolute head of our household. My outspokenness often landed me in hot water with the bishop, but because of my convert status, I was usually given a slap on the wrist and put back on the straight path. One day, the bishop called Dee into his office for a meeting, the gist of which was that Dee had better assert his position as head of the household and keep me in my place or there might be trouble. Dee told me later that he laughed at the bishop's remark and said, "If you want Clare in her place, then you better try to put her there yourself. I have to live with her."

Men are the overseers of women in the Mormon Church, since they have been charged with the task of perfecting and saving them, and so church programs are set up under priesthood authority in order to keep the women busy and involved. All organizations fall under the male priesthood, a change that came about during the "correlation" years in 1969 and 1970. Before that time, as I understand it, the Relief Society had been relatively autonomous.

I joined the church just as this new "correlation" program was being phased in. From listening to some of the sisters in the Lorain ward, many were not happy about having this one final piece of independence yanked out from under them and placed under the watchful eye of the priesthood.

I, like most of the women, participated in the various organizations including teaching the eleven-year-old boys in Primary, which was the scouting group. I have to admit, it was fun, and I learned a lot. I loved those boys, one of whom was my oldest son. I also served in various capacities in the Relief Society. One position was as a Visiting Teacher, a program in which the women went in pairs (a partner was assigned) once each month to visit an assigned group of five other "sisters" to check on them, make sure they weren't in need of anything, and report to the bishop any problems we detected.

One year my Visiting Teaching partner fell ill quite often. Although we were supposed to phone the Relief Society president and let her know we needed a substitute partner, often I didn't know my partner was unable to go until the last minute. Therefore, I would go alone. During these times, I believed the fact that I was an "outsider" gave the women I visited the courage to open up to me with their problems. This also gave me an opportunity to learn firsthand about the lack of power Mormon women have in their relationships with their husbands, and the devastating affect it has on their lives.

One "sister" I visited was a young woman about my age at the time—twenty-seven years old—who had a problem I had never heard of before; she was addicted to a drug called Valium. First, I did not have a clue to what Valium was or what it did. (I was not a pill taker and had trouble choking down vitamins or aspirin.) Second, when she told me that she was addicted, I thought she was kidding; there was no possible way that a "good" Mormon could be addicted to anything, except maybe going to church—certainly not to a drug of some kind!

"Sara" had been pressured into marriage by her family's and the church's expectations, even though she never really wanted to be married. One of the reasons she had not wanted to marry was her fear of sex. During her teenaged years, there had been a teacher in the church's Young Women's group who, in her overzealous attempt to keep her young charges pure and undefiled until their wedding day, had implanted in the minds of these girls the horrors of the sex act. It made an indelible impression on Sara. She never forgot what her teacher had told her. She developed such an aversion to sex that the mere thought of sex with a man nearly made her physically ill.

In her book, Sonia Johnson blames the church. "When to speak the names of the acts of sex or the sexual parts of the body is so powerfully taboo, it is little wonder there are so many sexual cripples in the church." I realized that Sara was indeed a sexual cripple.

Before Sara's marriage, three years before our conversation in the living room of her small apartment, she had gone to her family physician to talk to him about her fears. His solution: a prescription for Valium and instructions to take one each morning and one each evening before bedtime. It was a good remedy for awhile. It got her through the sex act each time her husband wanted it. She became pregnant. For nearly eight months, she used the pregnancy as an excuse not to have sex, and therefore did not have to take the Valium. After the baby was born, however, her husband resumed making sexual demands on her, and she called her doctor for another prescription.

By this time, two pills a day were not enough. Every time her husband put his arm around her, she froze, she told me, sobbing on my shoulder. Valium became her answer, and she discovered that her doctor would give her an unlimited supply. She was hooked. As she sat there, tears streaming down her cheeks, she begged me to help her. I was at a loss to know what to do.

I knew that my official duty was to report the situation to the bishop, yet she had told me her problems in strict confidence, and I could not betray her. I told her that she had to get help from a counselor, preferably a secular one at a mental health clinic somewhere in Salt Lake City where she would be less likely to be reported back to our bishop. I then prayed with her that she would have the strength she needed to overcome her addiction and the courage to do what ever she felt she had to with regard to her marriage. I just did not know what else to do. I found myself totally caught off guard by her "problem."

Not long after that incident, another "sister" confided in me that she too was addicted to a variety of medications I'd never heard of including Quaaludes, Percodan, and Percocet. By this time, I was familiar with Valium, but the rest were new ones to me. The woman's daughter had fallen seriously ill; more than a year later she had not regained consciousness. Mary had many physical problems herself, and so Mary's doctor prescribed the pills to help her keep her sanity through all her trials. Mary was hooked and she knew it. Like Sara, she had been given an unlimited prescription by her doctor.

Among women in Utah, addiction to drugs, both prescription and nonprescription, is an overwhelming problem. A report issued in 1980 by the State Division of Alcohol and Drugs showed that during an average month, there were roughly eighteen thousand users of nonprescription Amphetamines in the eighteen and over age group. A total of sixty-eight percent of Utah women used prescription drugs, and forty-nine percent reported using illegal drugs. Of the women using drugs of all types—legally prescribed, over-the-counter, and illegal—an average of 13.4 percent reported frequent or "heavy" (daily) use.

In September, 1987, *Utah Holiday* magazine published an article called *The Innocent Addiction*, by Marianne Burgoyne, which cited some revealing statistics. At that time, Utah ranked among the first five states in the nation in the purchase of easily abused drugs or narcotics. The state ranked third in the number of disciplinary actions per capita, other than revocations, taken against physicians, with eighty percent of these being drug related. Utahans used 3.3 percent of all methamphetamine prescribed yearly in the United States, yet the population of Utah at that time represented only seven tenths of a percent of the nation's total. (Diet pills are a big seller in Utah, where forty-eight percent of its women between the ages of twenty-five and forty-five are at least thirty percent overweight. At one of the annual Sunstone Conferences of "marginal" Mormons, a woman told of a friend of hers who had spoken with her bishop to confess her addiction to diet pills. "That's not a problem," he told her. "At least you're not fat like the rest of the sisters in the ward.")

Although the statistics did not break out the Mormon population of Utah, specifically, with Mormons making up the majority of Utah's population, the problem was obviously prevalent among Mormon women. If I personally knew of two in my ward of about 250 people, then surely there were more. Burgoyne quoted some local Salt Lake City pharmacists who called the prescription drug abuse problem in Utah the "Mormon Mommy complex," because so many Mormon women were on drugs to help them cope with the stresses of a pressure cooker society that demanded they be the perfect wife, mother, and all-around church worker. Yes, Mormons were high on life all right just like the *Reader's Digest* insert said, and perhaps methamphetamine and a few other prescription and nonprescription drugs. The problem is particularly disconcerting to me considering that Mormons have such strict laws concerning the ingesting of tea, coffee, and alcohol, rather innocuous "drugs" by comparison.

The problems of obesity, depression, and suicide were just as prevalent in Utah Mormon society as among the nation in general. The Osmond Family Syndrome produced a society of unhappy women, who hid behind smiling faces and denied that anything could possibly be wrong, while popping pills to make themselves feel better. A 1980 newspaper article, said that in Davis County (where Kaysville was located), depression was the leading mental health problem, according to then-director Russell Williams (who was also a member of my ward at the time). Dr. Williams stated that depression is often triggered by the failure to deal with problems—known as problem avoidance.

When I think about how actively the church was involved in trying to present to the world a perfect Mormon society that had no problems, it was no wonder that depression was so rampant due to problem avoidance. Problem avoidance was a way of life for the Mormon Church, so why should it not be among its members?

Suicide among women in Utah is also a problem. Recently, a friend (who was raised Mormon, but is no longer a member) told me her sister called in tears over the suicide of her best friend. Carrie's sister, who lives in a small town in southern Utah, was thirty-two years old and had eight children. Her friend had been about the same age and also had eight children. Unable to take the pressure of being the perfect wife, mother, and church worker, she had chosen to end her life. Now Carrie's sister was wondering if she should not do the same (kill herself), since, as she told Carrie, "I'm not a very good mother either." I saw much depression among my female friends, which often led them to a doctor's office and, subsequently, to a quick fix of Valium or some other drug.

Yet, the rationalization seemed to be that "if a doctor prescribed it, it must be okay for me." In addition, women were programmed to believe male priesthood holders knew best. Since most of their doctors fell into this category, women believed they were doing nothing wrong. They were accustomed to being submissive and taking advice from men, so following a doctor's prescription, even to the point of addiction, was some-how rationalized as okay. I became angry at the thought that these men were blatantly keeping many women drugged to the point of addiction, thus preventing any addressing of the real problems women faced, whether it were obesity, fear of sex, or stress due to the problems of too many children and too little time. That these women took so many drugs seemed to fly in the face of Mormon teachings about keeping one's body in good health, a doctrine called the Word of Wisdom.

9
৪৩৫৩

Word of Wisdom?

$\mathcal{M}$y experiences during my Visiting Teaching sessions, along with my own investigations into the problem of drug abuse in Utah, prompted me to question the Mormon doctrine called the Word of Wisdom. One of the problems with religious legalism is that it leads to hairsplitting, and that is especially true with this particular law. Is taking four Valium per day more "moral" than having a glass of wine just because a doctor prescribed the Valium? Is drinking Coke or Pepsi more moral than drinking coffee or tea just because there is no law against Coke or Pepsi—even though both contain caffeine? Isn't the reason for the ban against tea and coffee the chemical caffeine, which is contained in those substances? Isn't caffeine caffeine, no matter what form it takes? What about the caffeine in certain painkillers such as Excedrin? I began to question the whole of Mormon dogma, starting with the absurdities of the doctrine of the Word of Wisdom.

The Word of Wisdom is the most visible rule in the Mormon Church. It is the most-often talked about "law" for good Mormons and the most joked about by non- and jack-

Mormons. Much in Utah Mormon society, including its liquor laws at that time, is a reflection of this rule. Utah is an extremely legalistic society in terms of religious law. No rule among the Mormons is so strongly adhered to by good Mormons—and blatantly ignored by non- and jack-Mormons—as the Word of Wisdom. It is a problematic law, however, because it is such a common standard by which the church judges its members, that it is used by members as a yardstick to measure the righteousness of their neighbors. (This is often problematic in legalistic religions.)

This "law" actually started out as a piece of good advice, given by Joseph Smith through a "revelation" from God to help the Mormons be healthy people. The law, found in the book of the Doctrine and Covenants, says, "That inasmuch as any man drinketh wine or strong drink among you, behold it is not good, . . . strong drinks are not for the belly, but for the washing of your bodies. And again, tobacco is not for the body, neither for the belly, and is not good for man, but is an herb for bruises and all sick cattle, to be used with judgment and skill. And again, hot drinks are not for the body or belly." (D&C 89:5-10) The church interpreted hot drinks as being tea and coffee. This "advice" is now a strict law upon which hangs every Mormon's eternal life. Strict obedience to the Word of Wisdom became part of the criteria for entering the temple in the early part of this century. Breaking of this law means that one is not entitled to a temple recommend, which in turn means that, technically, members could be denied entrance into the Celestial Kingdom and association with family in the afterlife just because they had a cup of coffee for breakfast, or a glass of iced tea with lunch, wine with dinner, or because they smoked cigarettes.

I never had a problem with the Word of Wisdom because it encourages a healthy lifestyle. I never smoked, and although I sometimes drank tea, coffee, or alcohol before my conversion, I had no problem giving them up. Where I started running into problems with the Word of Wisdom was when I began to see the way Mormons used the rule as an end unto itself rather than a means to an end, i.e., good health. The idea that tea and coffee are bad for one's health is due to the caffeine, which poses additional problems.

If the intent of the advice was to prevent the ingestion of caffeine via tea and coffee, then did it not stand to reason that all substances containing caffeine should be banned? From time to time, some Mormons have asked the General Authorities to rule in that direction, however, the answer has always been that it is not good to "command" in all things. I knew some Mormons who strictly adhered to the "rule" and would not drink hot chocolate or use chocolate chips in cookies, nor would they drink any soft drink containing caffeine. Others, however, claiming that only those substances named specifically by church officials were taboo, partook freely of caffeine-laden soft drinks and chocolate. Therein lies one of the major problems with religious legalism: if there is a commandment against one thing, then there must be commandments for all things. If there are commandments in one specific area, then there must be commandments to cover the "gray" areas, in this case the soft drink and chocolate issue.

After I started my office job in 1978, I began having a cup of coffee each morning at the office. We had a coffee maker there, and it was convenient. I enjoyed the good taste of a cup of coffee. I often received frowns from those of my coworkers who were Mormon—who knew I was also—as I walked by, cup in hand. Then off they would go to the soda machine in the break room to line up for their morning jolt of Coca-Cola or Pepsi, which contained caffeine just like my coffee. Most of them drank Coke or Pepsi all day. Still, they could take smug satisfaction in the fact that they could qualify for a temple recommend and I could not. Another problem that arises when commandments only partially cover an issue, is that people develop a holier-than-thou attitude. By this time, I no longer had a temple recommend anyway, so it didn't matter to me, but the attitude of my coworkers really made me angry.

I found the obsession that Mormons have with the Word of Wisdom a strange thing. It became harder for me to deal with the attitude that many Mormons who keep this law acquired. The Word of Wisdom definitely separates the spiritual "haves" from the "have nots" in Utah. I had a friend who thought nothing of bad-mouthing people who drink tea or coffee, because she drank only Tab diet soft drink. She drank it every day— all day—from morning until night. In fact, she took great care to be sure she had enough on hand so she would not run out. If by chance she did run out, and it was Sunday, she would break the church's rules about shopping on the Sabbath to go buy her Tab. I found it amusing that her own addiction to this cola drink was completely lost to her, and she failed to see the intent of the law over the letter of the law. She was keeping the letter of the law, but was totally failing in its intent. Mormonism, however, is a religion that is much more concerned with letter than intent when it comes to obedience to its rules and regulations.

My next door neighbor was a widow woman in her seventies, who used to fix a pot of coffee each morning, have her two cups, then open all the windows to air out the house just in case anyone from the church—especially the bishop—came to visit. She really worried that someone from the ward would find out that she drank coffee. One day I asked if she didn't think God had better things to do than worry about whether or not she was drinking coffee.

"Yes, I do," she replied with a chuckle. "But the people around here don't, and they're the ones that count right now."

Her daughter came to live with and care for her during my last summer in Utah prior to my leaving the state, bringing her husband and teenaged children. One evening, while I was sitting on my front porch looking at the beautiful mountains and especially Francis Peak, which stood like a sentinel over Kaysville, my neighbor's fourteen-year-old granddaughter came to visit me. Her father was a good man, however, he was a jack Mormon who drank coffee and smoked cigarettes. She expressed concern for her father's soul.

"I worry that we'll never see my father again after we all die because he doesn't keep the Word of Wisdom," she said to me.

"Do you really believe that God would deny your father the pleasure of being with his family just because of coffee and cigarettes?" I asked her.

She nodded yes. So, I began talking with her about how Jesus was often reprimanded by the religious leaders of his day for failing to follow all the rules and regulations. Jesus rebuked those men and told them they were more concerned about what men did on the outside than what they were on the inside. "It's not what people put into themselves that defiles them," I told her "but what comes out of a person's heart that makes them bad." (Matthew 15:10-20)

I tried to explain to her that the God I worshipped and loved was a loving God who would forgive and judge fairly and justly, because God looks at the heart. Only man looks at the outward acts of another person and judges, and that is wrong, I explained to her. She seemed somewhat relieved after our conversation, and I hope that she remembered our talk. Her comments made me realize how the critical, judgmental nature of Mormonism can destroy people rather than build them up. Even this young girl knew her father was an outcast in Mormonism just because he didn't live the Word of Wisdom. But she also believed he was a good man, and she couldn't reconcile that kind of "punishment" for something so totally unrelated to a person's spirituality as drinking coffee or smoking cigarettes.

It was very common for non-Mormons or jack Mormons to smoke. It was almost like wearing a badge that said, "NO, I'm NOT a Mormon!" Both of my best friends at work smoked. One was a jack Mormon, who had been practically disowned from her family for many years, and the other was a non-Mormon who had lived in Utah only a few years after her husband's company transferred him there. After I asked her why she always made it a point to smoke so much in public, my non-Mormon friend said, "I don't want people mistaking me for a Mormon!"

Whether or not one keeps the Word of Wisdom is visible. As a result, *that* more than any other (aside from having lots of children) has become a symbol for Mormonism, and the thing that differentiates the "good" Mormons from the "marginal" or jack Mormons. Mormons living on the fringes of the religion who smoke, drink tea, coffee, or alcohol, see the overcoming of those "habits" as their one ticket back into the church.

I ran into a woman—a member of my ward—in the grocery store one day. She had a carton of cigarettes in her shopping cart. When she saw me, she attempted to cover it up with a box of cereal. However, she knew that I had seen them.

"These are my husband's," she said, looking embarrassed. "He's trying to quit smoking and drinking beer so he can start coming to church again, but it's really hard for him."

I felt badly that she felt the necessity to justify the carton of cigarettes to me. After all, who was I? I was not her or her husband's judge. Later, I realized that her fear of running into me in the store while she had cigarettes in her cart was justified. In Utah Mormon society, everyone is set up to be everyone else's judge. It is not intentional nor an official "calling" but another consequence of the legalistic, hierarchical, and patriarchal structure of the Mormon Church. Everyone is thrust into a position of being a watchdog over everyone else. I could certainly see the good intent in the Visiting Teaching and Home Teaching[27] programs. I think, for the most part, the official intentions are noble. Too often these good intentions, when combined with the power of the male priesthood, create a system that encourages "snitching." Many fringe Mormons saw it as prying into their private lives. Some refused to allow Home Teachers or Visiting Teachers into their homes. When people are put into positions of power and authority over other people, and given yardsticks with which to measure others, the boundary between true caring and holier-than-thou prying is often blurred.

This woman's comment was interesting from another standpoint. She took pains to point out to me that as soon as her husband quit drinking beer and smoking, he would come back to church. Although church authorities would deny—and rightly so—that there are any rules against a person coming to church who is not keeping the Word of Wisdom, I can understand why someone who is not marching in lockstep with good Mormons would feel uncomfortable and out of place. That is a shame. The well need no physician, yet for those Mormons who are spiritually ailing in Utah, for those Mormons who are not keeping all the rules, there is no place in the church. If there is no place for them within the church, then there is certainly no place outside the church—they believe—in which they will be accepted either. I quickly understood just how fringe members felt. I often thought, during the years I spent in Utah as a "good" Mormon, that I would never want to be out of tune with Utah

---

27 Home Teaching is similar to Visiting Teaching, except that two elders are assigned two families to visit each month during the evening when the entire family is present to give them a short lesson and see if there are any needs in the family. They then report back to the bishop any needs or concerns.

Mormon society, because I knew that life—especially in a small town—would be very lonely. In a homogeneous place like Kaysville, there would be nowhere to hide. I would soon find out that my perceptions were correct.

I consider the Word of Wisdom to be good advice, as it was intended. Adhering to it probably means better physical health. Using this law as a means by which to measure a person's worth, or to judge a person's worthiness to participate in church activities, or to obtain a temple recommend, however, is to my way of thinking, detrimental to one's spiritual health. It is certainly not in line with my interpretations of true Christianity in any way, shape, or form. I saw too many people spiritually devastated and left without hope because they could not keep the Word of Wisdom.

Most Mormons who have been brought up in that religion truly believe that because the church deems them unacceptable to participate in the life of the ward or "unworthy" to go to the temple, that this somehow also makes them "unacceptable" or "unworthy" as people in the eyes of God. When confronted with this, the only thing I could do for them was point out the New Testament scripture about which I spoke with my neighbor's granddaughter. However, I am not sure that anyone believed me, because Mormons are taught to doubt the veracity of the Bible.

This obsession with the vital importance of keeping the Word of Wisdom was evident on Sunday also. During the ten years I attended the Mormon Church it was the most common topic of the talks given. The importance of keeping this law was pounded into our heads repeatedly. Toward the end of my life as a Mormon, I began wondering if there weren't more pressing issues in the life of the Mormon Church than whether its members drank tea or coffee, or smoked cigarettes. Most of the people sitting in the pews on Sunday were those who kept that rule anyway, so it seemed to me that all that preaching was lost on people who did not need to hear it anyway.

Perhaps the point was to make those in the pews on Sunday feel good about themselves—a little gloating over the fact that they were adhering to the Word of Wisdom. Perhaps the church felt that by keeping the people focused on such trivial external matters, it kept them distracted from the far more important internal "spiritual" matters. The importance placed on the Word of Wisdom often overshadowed weightier issues of society such as that of spouse abuse, child abuse, and adultery, which were seldom talked about from the pulpit. Issues of faith and faith development often meant little more than faith in the Mormon Church and its leaders. Very few talks I heard had any real theological significance. Theology means very little to most Mormons, who depend on the church leadership to provide for them all they need to know about scripture.

10
୧୦୧୨

Mormon Theology: Right and Wrong

Theology has always been important to me in my life. I love studying not only scriptures but anything connected with religious history, so it was only natural that studying both Mormon history and Mormon scriptures became a big part of my life after I joined the Mormon Church. Church leaders encourage study of the Book of Mormon, much more so than study of the Bible, and I diligently attended these "scripture" study sessions that were routinely held each week in various members' homes. I really tried with all my heart and soul to understand Mormon theology. I came to learn that it is so complicated and convoluted, that the more in depth one gets the more confusing it becomes. If Mormons appeared to have all the answers at first, it became apparent to me after a few years that Mormon theology—at least for those who cared enough to go into it in depth—merely creates more questions.

Mormon theology consists of a basic belief in "theodicy" or the belief that God returns good for good and evil for evil, a premise that can be traced back to very early Old Testament times when people saw God as a harsh judge who meted out punishment for wrong doings and rewards for doing good. That is not always how it works, however. We know from observing life that bad things happen to good people and good things happen to bad people. (Read the book of Job, which put Old Testament theodicy to the test.)

One evening during scripture study class we were discussing this principal—that if one is living all the laws of the gospel (according to Mormon belief) then one will be rewarded, and vice versa. I posed an experiential question to the group challenging this belief:

"What if someone does things against the laws of God and still is rewarded?" I asked. "For example, I can remember when I was about nineteen, going out on Saturday night, getting very drunk, and driving home on those winding, dark-as-pitch, country roads in Kentucky. I would wake up the next morning, unable to remember how I got home and into bed safely. If God rewards goodness and punishes bad behavior, then why did He guide me home safely instead of causing me to run up a telephone pole?"

Immediately, one man in the group had the answer—he usually had all the answers and apparently had pondered this question before: "You obviously had done enough good things that you hadn't been rewarded for, so that the fact that you were drunk didn't count yet."

I looked at him in utter disbelief. God keeps this big score card, and one side is listed all the good things a person does, and the other side lists is all the bad. If one has more good than bad, then one is ahead. "Oh," I said. "God owed me one."

This man nodded, smiling broadly, proud of his tremendous theological insight. "Well," I continued. "Then how does a person know when it's even-Steven and you might get punished the next time you do wrong?" That was a stumper. He thought about it for a minute and then said, "That's why you always have to do good. You never know when the score is even."

Among Mormons, I discovered, there is a warped sense of right and wrong, despite a belief among them that right and wrong are two very clear-cut ideas as different as black and white or night and day. Religious legalism often spawns this skewed sense of right and wrong, and nowhere I have ever lived has it been more skewed than in Utah Mormon society. For example, in the late 1970s a study was conducted—I believe by a University of Utah sociology group—of Utah's teenage population. Surveys were sent out to high-school-aged youth that questioned them on many of the religious taboos held by Mormons. One of the questions dealt with smoking and drinking alcohol. As I recall, the results of the survey proved that an extremely low number of young people did either, indicating a strong adherence to the Word of Wisdom.

However, on the matter of being sexually active, the percentages were quite high, something like sixty percent of sixteen- and seventeen-year-olds were sexually active. Regarding the use of protection to prevent pregnancy: less than ten percent of the sexually active teenagers used any protection. Next came a question asking which was the greater sin, smoking cigarettes, or being sexually active, or using birth control while sexually active. Most all the teenagers answered that smoking was a greater sin than being sexually active and that practicing birth control was next. The results of the survey indicated more proof of the tremendous impact that the Word of Wisdom had on Utah's population. That keeping the Word of Wisdom was more spiritually important than sexual purity was apparent in the statistics provided by the Utah Department of Health report that showed a steady increase in the number of out-of-wedlock births from 1970 through 1984. There were 2,958 out-of-wedlock births in 1984, with 1,093 of those in the fifteen to nineteen age bracket.

Another example of skewed reasoning about right and wrong is evident among many Mormon men. The patriarchal structure of Mormonism seems much more overpowering in Utah where there is a high concentration of Mormons. Mormonism is a religion that gratifies the male ego, enhances the idea of male superiority to the female, and reinforces the age-old idea that women are the property of their husbands. This comes from Old Testament times, when a man's wives were listed among his other possessions such as sheep, goats, cattle, and lands. Although mainstream Mormonism forbids the practice of polygamy, it is a well-known and accepted belief that in the next life, when a man reaches godhood, he will have an abundance of wives.

Because this idea of eternal polygamy is always present in the belief system of Mormon men, there is a tendency for them to look upon all women they encounter in this life as potential sexual partners. One woman told me once that a "good" Mormon man, her supervisor at work and a member of the bishopric in his ward, was after her continually. He kept promising her it was okay for them to have an affair because he had already designated her as one of his wives-to-be in the next life, suggesting they could get a jump on the process by consummating the union in this life. He said he did not even care if she got pregnant because that would prove her fertility and ability to produce him many "spirit children" in eternity.

Eugene England, who teaches English at Brigham Young University, wrote about the idea of eternal polygyny in an article for *Dialogue: A Journal of Mormon Thought*, (an alternative quarterly literary/historical magazine not sanctioned by church officials). "It does not seem reasonable to me that God would require polygyny, with all its attendant problems, simply to reduce time [that it would take to populate a world such as this one] by giving each man four or six wives. If humans can already produce test-tube babies and clones, God has certainly found more efficient ways to produce spirit children than by turning celestial partners into mere birth machines. To anticipate such a limited, unequal role for women in eternity insults and devalues them."

However, Mormon women, especially in Utah, are seen primarily as reproducers whose sole value is their ability to have children, stay at home, and nurture them while waiting on their husbands. Men, with their enhanced status as the "saviors of their wives" are valued for their priesthood powers and come close to being worshipped here on earth, as if their godhood status were already conferred upon them. Indeed it is, as the cloak of the priesthood gives men the "authority to act for God."

Mormon women, especially in Utah, will never achieve equal footing with men. Despite pressures from the more liberal, vocal women who are calling for priesthood ordination for women, they will never gain that right; it has in recent years been called a "moot point" by church leaders. Thus, men hold a revered status in Mormonism that places them far above women and affects their dealings with women in this life. England, in his *Dialogue* article, "On Fidelity," stated that he sees a problem with the "dubious argument" that celestial polygyny will work just because "we will be morally superior there, more able to love inclusively. Such an expectation can tempt us to love inclusively and superficially—even promiscuously—in this life."

Skewed thinking, in terms of right and wrong, which is so prevalent in the sexual attitudes of Mormon males—especially those in Utah (or in other heavily populated Mormon areas such as Mesa, Arizona)—often shows up in deviant forms of sexual behavior. In about 1994, a male Mormon Sunday school teacher in Mesa, Arizona, was arrested and accused of sexually abusing a teenage girl. The forty-three-year-old man allegedly undressed a fifteen-year-old girl and fondled her during a nude photo session in which he promised to make her a model. The man then called her several more times asking her for additional nude photo sessions. According to a newspaper account, the man told the girl he would not have sex with her "because he was married."

In October 1992, two dentists practicing in Spanish Fork, Utah, and who were twin brothers, had their licenses suspended for unprofessional conduct after it was found that one of the brothers had sex with a drug-addicted female patient while she was in their office. One of the brothers, a former Mormon bishop, admitted allowing the woman to perform a sex act on him during an office visit, according to a newspaper account. He also admitted to taking lewd photographs of the woman while she was in the dental chair and under the sedative gas nitrous oxide. His license was suspended for four years. The other brother, former mayor of Spanish Fork, admitted giving the woman the narcotic painkiller Demerol during one visit, at which time she gave him lewd photographs of herself, although she denied that the photos were in exchange for the drugs. His license was suspended for thirty days.

I knew several Mormon men who were engaged in extramarital affairs (which they justified using the "practicing for the next life" excuse). The best example was a good friend (non-Mormon) in Arizona who, after her divorce, began a five-year-long affair with a Mormon man who had a wife and three children. At the time he began the affair with her, she knew nothing about Mormonism. When I met her and we became friends, they had been together about three years. She expressed to me her hopefulness that one day he would leave his wife and marry her. She was obviously madly in love with him and told me what a great lover he was. She was addicted to sex with him, which they enjoyed twice a week, usually Wednesday night and all day on Saturday. She often traveled with him on business as well.

When she told me about this man, I warned her not to get her hopes up. Because he was a Mormon, there would be many barriers to her ever getting him as a husband. Over the course of several months, I was able to explain Mormon doctrine to her to help her better understand where her married lover was coming from and how his theology might affect their relationship. She began to see his behavior as hypocritical. She even told me that he left her house earlier than usual one Saturday evening after their standard all-day tryst, to go to the Mormon Stake Center and baptize a nephew.

She began talking with him about the possibility of his leaving his wife, but all he would promise her was that in the next life, she would be the first woman he would "call forth" (after his wife, of course) to be one of his polygamous wives. When I explained that theology to her, she decided that perhaps she had better end the relationship, which she did. He tried to talk her out of it by telling her that if it wasn't her, it would be some other woman, since he had to have a mistress, but she was unswayed. To this day, even though she has remarried, she thinks of him often and misses him terribly, a testimony to the powerful salesmanship skills of so many of these men.

Although I believed most of the men in Kaysville to be good, hardworking men who only wanted the best for their wives, children, and community, some of them had egos that were just too much to take. They had already become gods in their own mind. I had several good friends whose husbands walked about three feet off the ground at all times. I took much pleasure in baiting them with a kind of pseudo-patronization, watching them puff up with pride, like little bantam roosters, not even realizing that I was being facetious. The thought of having to spend eternity under the authority of any one of these men absolutely nauseated me.

The patriarchal structure that gives Mormon males absolute authority over their wives and children also sets the stage for spouse and child abuse, which the church continues to deal with only superficially in its meetings through "talks" urging men to be kind and loving toward their families. Yet, they do nothing to alter the theological structure—the powerful patriarchal priesthood-authoritative hierarchy—that forms a solid basis for much of the abuse. Although officially the church counsels men to rule their families in love, some men, when given the kind of power the priesthood offers, tend to take it to extremes.

Several of my friends actually cowered before their husbands and did what they were told unquestioningly to avoid confrontation. The men were no fools either; they knew they wielded that sort of power over their wives. One friend, April, was a sweet person—soft-spoken, rather bashful, but a lot of fun when she wasn't around her husband who intimidated her terribly with his "I know better than you, so shut-up" attitude. When he said, "jump" April would ask, "how high." She waited on him hand and foot and endured his rages when things were not going right. Although they were married "properly" in the temple, he rarely attended church, and April was the only one who still wore her temple garments. Still, he was well aware of his priesthood "authority" and took that part of his life quite seriously when it came to lording it over his wife and three children. Although I never saw him hit her, it would not surprise me if he had. Like most of the women in Kaysville, April had married young, had no education beyond high school, and no job experience. Out of necessity for financial support, these women stayed in situations that were tolerable at best.

I will hand it to one of my friends, who remains my friend to this day. Although her husband never really liked me or

approved of my outspoken, unsubmissive ways, she and I became very close friends. She stuck by me to the bitter end, when
nearly everyone else in the ward had deserted me. I am sure she
did this against the advice of or maybe even the command from
her husband that she not associate with me lest she risk her own
standing in the church. In spite of him, she maintained our
friendship—for which I will always be grateful.

One of the reasons I would later leave Utah was the thought
of ever being single there and having to date any of the men.
Dee may not have been perfect, and we had our share of ups and
downs, but he always let me be my own person and never even
pretended that we were anything less than equal partners.

Looking back on it now, I am certain that Dee never believed much of Mormon doctrine even though he tried to become a good Mormon. Although it was his idea to return to the
fold, I believe that he did not buy into the program even as
much as I did. He really did not want the burden of being any
one's "savior" and probably never believed he could be anyway.
I'm sure that becoming a god was something that he did not
want.

After we left Utah in 1981, he never again went to church.
Today, he professes no formal religious belief system. That is
the way it is with many ex-Mormons (and there are MANY ex-
Mormons, despite the church's official denial of that fact). Once
they leave the fold, there is no church, no religion, no God. It
stands to reason that if the "only true church" on earth is no
longer true, then surely everything is false. Many fall into a state
of total disbelief in anything remotely connected with church or
organized religion. It is a sad commentary and a testament to
what results when a religion preaches "conditional" love to its
adherents: When the conditions are not met, there is no love.

11

୫୦ଓଔ

Mormon Theology: Conditional Love

Conditional love runs deeply through the roots of Mormonism. Although Mormons outwardly preach love, their practice of it is limited primarily to fellow Mormons who live in the approved and accepted way. To love those outside the realm of Mormonism, or those with different color skin or religious beliefs, is difficult for most Utah Mormons, many of whom have never been exposed to the outside world. In an attempt to explain certain things such as why some people are black, Mormon doctrine—naturally—has an answer. The "descendants of Cain" theory is accepted. But as it was explained to me, those who were born black failed to be obedient and keep all the commandments in their "first estate" the heaven where spirits reside prior to coming to inhabit earthly bodies of flesh and blood. Their punishment was to be born black, or born Asian, or born in a communist country, or born in poverty. All were outward signs, according to Mormon doctrine, that a person failed to be as diligent and obedient in heaven as he could have been.

Being born Caucasian, in the United States, and to well-off parents—especially if those parents were Mormon—meant that you had kept your first estate extremely well. The degree to which you are good or bad in the first estate (in the spirit world) determines the lot you draws in this life. When I learned this, it made sense to me. Much of Mormon theology, on the surface, appears logical, and this seemed to be a simple answer to what is a very complex question. (Mormons had simple answers to everything because everything *had* to have an answer. No question could be left unanswered because that might cause someone to think, try to come up with his or her own answer. In Mormonism, uniformity of thought is crucial to membership in the church.)

The Book of Mormon teaches that Native Americans were given red skin because of a fight between two brothers who were among the first settlers to the Americas, two Jewish men who left the Middle East and floated to Central America in a submarine-type water craft. The "good" brother remained white, while the "bad" brother and his descendants were cursed by God with a red skin so one could tell the good guys from the bad guys, so to speak. The Book of Mormon teaches that the only way that a Native American has any hope of salvation is by joining the Mormon Church, which after a few generations will result in the skin becoming "white and delightsome."[28]

I questioned this idea of people's skin having to change color before they could be accepted by God, but I learned early

---

28   After the rule was changed about blacks holding the priesthood, the statements in the Book of Mormon concerning the Lamanites becoming a "white and delightsome" people were altered in 1981 to read "a pure and delightsome" people. Although Mormons say that their Book of Mormon no longer says "white," I still have my earlier edition which reads "white." It would seem that this is one instance where their scripture, which they claim is the most correctly translated book of scripture in existence, is not so correct after all.

in my Mormon journey that questioning church doctrine was not acceptable. Doing so called into question one's fealty to the church leaders, to whom absolute obedience and loyalty is required as a condition of remaining a member in good standing. At nearly every conference of the church which was held the first weekend each October and April, members were warned to follow their church leaders without fail, because "members place their souls in danger when they criticize their religious leaders or church teachings," said Elder James E. Faust, a member of the church's Council of Twelve Apostles. As a result questioned church doctrine in my own mind at first; I questioned the belief that only white citizens of the United States who were also Mormons were favored by God.

African Americans could be members of the church but could not be members of the priesthood, which was reserved for white male members only. In Bruce McConkie's *Mormon Doctrine* he states: "Negroes in this life are denied the priesthood; under no circumstances can they hold this delegation of authority from the Almighty... The gospel message of salvation is not carried affirmatively to them . . . The Negroes are not equal with other races where the receipt of certain spiritual blessings are concerned, particularly the priesthood and the temple blessings that flow therefrom, but this inequality is not of man's origin. It is the Lord's doing . . . "[29]

When the word came down on June 9, 1978 that Spencer W. Kimball, prophet of the church, had a revelation concerning African-American men and the priesthood, which stated that henceforth, all eligible and worthy black males could hold the Mormon priesthood, it was a shocking revelation. The world

---

29   Don't try looking for these references in the latest editions of either the Book of Mormon or McConkie's *Mormon Doctrine*, as the church has removed all references to the former status of African Americans from its official doctrine.

outside Utah hailed the revelation as a wonderful event, a break-through for African Americans and a sign that the old theological barriers of Mormonism were being broken down. Inside Utah however, such was far from the truth. In a small town like Kaysville, Utah where there were no black people at all, there was much prejudice against people of color, and understandably so. For more than one-hundred years the Mormon Church had been preaching doctrine that stated that people of color were inferior. That meant there were at least four generations that had been systematically indoctrinated with prejudice as a basic tenet of their religious beliefs. Overnight, these people were supposed to accept and welcome into the fold a group of people who for more than one hundred years had been "unacceptable."

Suddenly, what had been spoken as the "truth" (which in Mormonism means something unchangeable—"what is true today was true yesterday and will be true tomorrow") was changed and was no longer truth. There was a new "truth." And people—at least my friends and neighbors in Kaysville—were not buying it. Some were angry about the change and vowed they would never accept it (and some probably haven't to this day).

In claiming to have absolute truth, Mormon doctrine creates an inherent problem; in reality, there is nothing "absolute" about Mormon doctrine. Of course, Mormonism tries to cover its bases by telling its adherents that listening to the current prophet and president of the church is the most important thing in determining the "truth." Mormons are taught not to consider changes in church doctrine to be changes in truth, merely new revelations, which override old revelations. The present-day prophet's advice and revelations are the most current, up-to-date admonitions and take precedence over any previous rules or doctrines.

For many years, Mormons had the Lamanite program, named after that group of people described in the Book of Mormon as the first tribe of red-skinned people to inhabit the Americas. One Lamanite program, the Indian Student Placement program, was an attempt to help the Native American people become "white and delightsome" by removing Native American children from the reservations at the age of eight and placing them in foster homes with good Mormon families to be educated and reared in the Mormon way until they were eighteen. Many Native Americans participated in this program and willingly gave their children to the church so they would have the opportunity to receive an education and a chance at a better way of life.

The program always had its detractors and controversy swirled around this plan throughout its life. I knew many families in Kaysville that had a "Lamanite" son or daughter living with them, and sometimes it worked out well; sometimes it didn't. The culture shock was often too much for some of these youngsters, yanked from their desert homes on remote reservations.

Others became so homesick they became physically ill and had to be returned to their families. Stories circulated about a family that used a Lamanite youngster as nothing more than a slave to do the chores and help out with all the other children in the family.

I was never convinced of the prudence of this program. After a firsthand experience with the program, I became firmly convinced that the church was attempting nothing less than cultural genocide for these youngsters. I was known for my writing and speaking abilities, so a friend of mine who was in charge of the Lamanite speech festival for Davis County called me to see if I would participate as a judge, and I agreed.

The following Saturday at the local high school, I went to my assigned room where I would hear and judge the speeches of a dozen sixteen-year-old Native Americans. They were seated in a row on the stage. One by one they came to the podium and gave their prepared speeches. One very thin, Navajo girl stepped to the podium. She stood looking at her audience with huge, dark eyes that dominated her unusually fine facial features. She had a frightened, deer-caught-in-the-headlights look about her.

Slowly, she started her speech. It was about her grandmother. Raised by her grandmother, she was taken from her home at age twelve and brought to Utah to live with a Mormon family. Her speech was heart wrenching. Homesickness had been her companion for four years. She missed her grandmother; she missed her life on the reservation in the wild openness of the desert. Then the most crushing blow of all: her grandmother had died earlier that year. Though she begged and pleaded, the church had refused to let her go back to the reservation for her grandmother's traditional Native American burial ceremony.

Tears streamed down her face as she related her story. Those in charge of the program knew of her desperate homesickness and thought that letting her return even for a few days might cause the girl more pain than she could stand. They also had been afraid that she would run away and not return to the program. By the time she was finished speaking, I was in tears. I could not believe that church officials had been so heartless with the child that they put their selfish interests ahead of the emotional well-being of this girl.

I will never forget her face as long as I live. I told my friend who was in charge of the festival about the girl and asked her if we should contact someone about the girl's emotional state. I had written down her name so I wouldn't forget it. But my friend said it was best to stay out of the middle of what could be a negative controversy. I listened to her, but have always regretted not trying to help this young girl.

In recent years the Lamanite programs have been phased out or drastically cut back. One of the biggest critics of the church's increasing disinterest in Native Americans was George P. Lee, the first and only Native American to serve as a General Authority as a member of the First Quorum of Seventy since his appointment in 1975. Lee was stripped of his church membership on September 2, 1989 for "apostasy" and "other conduct unbecoming a member of the church." He claimed in a statement issued to the *Salt Lake Tribune* shortly after his excommunication that the church leaders had "turned their backs" on Native Americans and were discriminating against them. In letters written to the General Authorities, Lee accused the church leaders of "an attitude of superior race, white supremacy, racist attitude, pride, arrogance, and love of power." He accused them of "putting conditions" on their love for him. Lee discovered what many of us eventually come to know: Mormonism is a religion of conditional love.

Utah Mormonism promotes racism, perhaps not intentionally, but under the surface. Believing they are theologically and religiously superior, Mormons also believe—as they have been taught—that they are racially superior. There was never any doubt in my mind that in spite of outward efforts to be acceptable to all people by appearing to accept all people, Utah Mormons remain to this day some of the most prejudiced people I know.

Not only do people of color feel the sting of Mormon prejudice, but Mormons also shun gays and lesbians because their sexual orientation is different. When I lived in Utah (and this was before homosexuals started coming out of the closet) homosexuality was never spoken of under any circumstances. Once I asked about homosexuals who might also be Mormon and what would happen to them if their sexual orientation were known. I was told that there were no homosexuals in

Mormonism. That is probably still true today for two reasons: If homosexuals are found out, they are promptly excommunicated, and if they wish to remain good Mormons they will keep their sexual orientation a secret. Thus, as far as the church is concerned, there are no Mormon homosexuals.

In 1984, Jan Cameron, of San Ramone, California, formed the support group HELP—Homosexual Education for Latter-day Parents, after finding out that her son was gay. She discovered that she was not the only Mormon parent of a gay person, but that reality was never discussed.

"My purpose wasn't to make waves," she said in an interview that appeared in the *Phoenix Gazette* in October, 1987, "but to make things easier for people who were struggling with this issue."

Another story profiled several homosexuals living in Arizona who are Mormons. "Carl" was a young man who was active in his ward as a Sunday school teacher and hoped he could keep his homosexuality a secret. He attended the support group Affirmation, a nationwide self-help organization for gay men and women who are active, inactive, or former members of the Mormon Church. Carl wanted to maintain his church membership and be an active participant, but acknowledged that it was difficult to keep his true beliefs a secret. (Isn't it strange that so many Mormons are forced to live with a "split consciousness?")

Marilyn, a woman in her forties, lost most of her family and her church membership when she announced her homosexuality. She spent twenty-two years of her life being the perfect Mormon wife and mother of four children, but deep down she was miserable. "I wasn't allowed to think. I couldn't say what I felt. I was emotionally abused by my husband," the article quoted her saying. "As he got older, he got meaner. But I wanted the marriage to work desperately. A good girl doesn't walk out of a marriage."

Then she discovered that she and the woman who was her best friend had been harboring the same, dark secret; they professed their love for one another. Marilyn went through a gut-wrenching divorce and was excommunicated from the church. Her former husband denounced her, and only two of her children stayed with her. She hopes that someday the church changes its belief that homosexuality is a sickness and a sin, which can be cured if repented of.

"Brad" exchanged his membership in the Mormon Church for peace of mind. "I couldn't continue my participation in a church that wouldn't accept me," he said. However he also said that he still feels that "the Mormon people are my people."[30]

Today, many more gay Mormons are coming out of the closet but want to remain Mormons. Although the church will not be able to ignore this segment of their membership forever, for now it maintains its stand that homosexuality is a sin that requires repentance. The days of pretending that homosexuals within the church do not exist are over. The church will be forced to find a way to accept these individuals as children of God as God created them.

However, the church continues to see many of these "fringe" groups as a threat. An Associated Press article quoted Boyd K. Packer, a church Apostle, as saying that "feminists, homosexuals and intellectuals are the three greatest dangers facing the Mormon Church today." If these people represent Mormonism's greatest dangers, then it doesn't speak well of a church that is supposed to be the only true church of God on the earth. Mormonism, when it shatters, will most certainly be destroyed from within and not from forces outside its walls.

---

30   Excerpted from "Belief vs. Gay Mormons" by Michelle Bearden for the *Phoenix Gazette*, October 10, 1987.

12

८०७३

Mormonism and Censorship

If racial and sexual prejudice were alive and well in Utah Mormonism, something equally insidious began to work its way into the fabric of Utah society during the late 1970s that caused me great alarm. There arose a group in Utah calling itself the "Citizens For True Freedom." It was founded by a woman in Ogden, Utah, just north of Kaysville. Joy Beech took up her cause with religious fervor. That cause was to rid the state of Utah of anything that smacked of pornography, as defined by her standards.

When I first heard of the group through some of my friends who had joined Beech's organization, the red warning lights went on in my head. Any group, I thought, that calls itself Citizens for True Freedom must be out to ensure its own freedom at the expense of curtailing the freedoms of others. I was right. She had set up community watchdog groups along the Wasatch front whose job it was to monitor all reading material in those communities. That meant books in libraries, magazines in stores, and even reading material on coffee tables in doctor's offices and beauty parlors.

In her efforts to rid the state of smut, nothing was sacred and no place off limits to Beech's attacks on the printed word. In some cases, according to newspaper accounts, neighbors even monitored each other's reading material. Some of her tactics included sending her then seventeen-year-old son into convenience stores to purchase *Playboy* or *Penthouse* magazines. If he was successful, all hell would break loose. However, I did not have as much problem with that as when she and her groupies began invading the public libraries.

She had a "hit" list of books, which she had deemed to be pornographic. CFTF people would go into their local library armed with the list and proceed to check out as many of the books as they could find. Then, in the name of protecting children from the evils of pornography, they "lost" the books. The list included any book written by Judy Blume in her series for teenagers and most things written by John Steinbeck, among others. Librarians were at their wits' end trying to keep an eye out for these people who might be checking out books just to destroy them.

Libraries and stores were not the only targets. So thorough was Beech's campaign that people were on the lookout for "pornography" everywhere. One day I heard there was a ruckus in downtown Kaysville near the beauty shop where I had my hair done every now and then. I went in the following Saturday to see what had happened. The girl that usually cut my hair said that some of the Citizens for True Freedom had come to the salon to confiscate various magazines. Their target had been all the *Cosmopolitan* magazines in the salon.

A woman under the hair dryer was looking through the magazines on the table next to her, trying to find something to read. Anyone who has ever seen a *Cosmopolitan* magazine knows that they have some pretty "racy" cover photos (racy by Utah standards, anyway). She picked one up and began thumbing through it to see just exactly to what sort of smut she was being exposed when she came across an article on female orgasm. That was it. After she was finished she went home, rallied some of her CFTF cohorts, and together they marched into the salon and began confiscating magazines right and left. Before the salon's owner could run them out, they had escaped with an armload of Cosmos and several others, taken them outside, and proceeded to burn them on the sidewalk. The police were called, several other merchants doused the flaming magazines, and the women were escorted away from the scene by Kaysville police.

I shook my head in disbelief. What kind of maniacal people would tread on the rights of others in the name of God and of course, the Mormon Church? And all over an article on female orgasm. I looked at my hairdresser and laughed, "Well, God forbid that any woman in Kaysville read about female orgasm! If any woman in this town ever had an orgasm there would be riots in the streets!" We laughed but knew that rampant censorship in Utah was no laughing matter. What I didn't know then, but would soon find out, was that censorship is promoted and practiced by Mormon Church officials, something that fanned the flames of Beech's zeal to use any method or means possible to control the minds of the people of Utah.

Ms. Beech, however, had found her true calling. She put a stop to Ogden school district's attempts to cooperate with the local humane society to encourage pet neutering by passing out pamphlets to school children, urging them to have their pets spayed or neutered. Beech took the position that children would think that if it were okay to spay and neuter a pet to prevent puppies or kittens, it would be equally okay to neuter people to prevent the birth of babies. Rather than fight her, the school district quit handing out the pamphlets.

Beech also tried to have a huge mural removed from the wall of the Western Airlines terminal (now Delta) at the Salt Lake International Airport. A renown Utah artist had been commissioned to paint the mural on the new terminal's interior wall opposite the escalators leading down into the baggage claim area. The mural depicted a man and woman against a sky with clouds floating around them. They were lying on their sides, the woman's back to the viewer with her head turned and lifted toward the sky and her arms outstretched. The man faced her in a position slightly above her, also with outstretched arms. The mural reminded me of something Rembrandt or Rubin would have painted during the Renaissance era. The flying couple was really quite a serene and beautiful painting and did not display any "improper" body parts. However, in a statement released by Beech when she attempted to have the airport authority remove it, she said that such pornography would "incite viewers of the painting to rape and murder." I, like many people, went to view the mural during the time it was receiving so much attention, and I experienced feelings from viewing the painting, however, rape and murder were not among them.

Beech blamed all society's ills on pornography, and said that sexually explicit magazines lead to sexual immorality and spread venereal diseases. Several letters to the editor of the *Salt Lake Tribune* appeared daily on the Beech subject. She became a daily topic of conversation among those few of us who considered her a danger to society. One person who wrote a letter was the founder of Survivors Network-Utah, a group of survivors of childhood sexual abuse. Robert L. Moore said, "In dealing with incest survivors on a daily basis for the past two years I have yet to talk with a lady from a home where pornography was available or condoned. They all are from strongly religious homes with a powerful, outwardly sexually repressive, patriarchal domination."

Censorship is an issue that looms large in Utah, something I didn't realize it until much later in my journey through Mormonism, and after I had started writing on a freelance basis for the Salt Lake daily newspapers. The extent to which censorship is condoned and practiced by the church is absolutely appalling for an organization whose basic tenets include "free agency" and an unwavering support of the United States Constitution. After Fawn Brodie, a professor and historian at a Southern California university, and a member of the church, wrote her now-infamous book, *No Man Knows My History*, a biography of Joseph Smith, the church's historical archives became more difficult to access. The reason was to prevent many of the true—and sometimes unfavorable—facts about Mormonism and its founders from reaching the ears of the church's faithful. Mormon authors Linda King Newell of Salt Lake City and Valeen Tippetts Avery of Flagstaff, Arizona, a professor and historian, wrote a book published by Doubleday in 1984 on Emma Smith, the wife of Mormon founder Joseph Smith. During their research in the historical archives of the church, the two discovered a very controversial figure in this woman whom had rarely been written about other than in the most positive light. According to an article that appeared in the Arizona Republic on August 18, 1984, when church leaders discovered that the book would contain some less-than-glowing images of the first prophet and his wife, the church denied the two writers further access to the documents in the archives, which they had, until that point, the freedom to peruse. The pair was even asked not to publish the book, after ten years of research.

In his article "On Being a Mormon Historian," D. Michael Quinn stated that, "In June 1986 the staff of the church historical department announced it was necessary to sign a form which Elder [Boyd] Packer declared gave the right of pre-publication censorship for any archival research completed before signing the form. I and several others refused to sign the form and have not returned to do research at LDS church archives since 1986." Failure to adhere to this rule often results in excommunication or being disfellowshipped. Quinn found, as I had some years earlier, the strange irony that exists in Mormonism that "the general authorities who praise free agency, also do their best to limit free agency's prerequisites—access to information, uninhibited inquiry, and freedom of expression."

Recently this issue exploded to the forefront when the church excommunicated or disfellowshipped several dissident writers and intellectuals in a mass purge in September of 1993, for speaking and writing on church-related subjects in a way that did not strictly follow church doctrine. The church has become almost paranoid about historians, writers, and other intellectuals who "colored outside the lines," so to speak, by questioning church doctrine, uncovering and revealing both the favorable and the unfavorable in church history.

Historians are urged to tell the selective truth about church history, or only those things that cast a favorable light upon the church, its history, its leaders, and its doctrines. Church Apostle Boyd Packer, a leader in the most recent purge, told Quinn in a 1976 interview for a position on the BYU faculty, that, "Historians should tell only that part of the truth that is inspiring and uplifting."[31]

The church is losing other intellectuals, also. Several BYU professors have been fired and others have resigned from their teaching positions over the church's restrictive policies. In October 1993, John Beck of Provo, Utah, resigned the church and quit his position as professor of business at BYU. "My

---

31   This is quoted from an article titled "Mormon Inquisition?" in the *Salt Lake City Messenger*, published by the Utah Lighthouse Ministry, Issue No. 85, Nov. 1993.

problems had to do with the ethics of the university," he said. His wife, Martha Nibley Beck, daughter of Hugh Nibley, a famous Mormon Church scholar and author of numerous books, left her position as a sociology professor at BYU after the university removed Carol Lee Hawkins as leader of the Women's Symposium . . . Martha Beck is quoted as saying that "The church is moving toward social isolation."[32]

A former public affairs liaison for the church, Paul Richards, who also left BYU, said, "The church wants to portray this image of being unified in all it does . . . It wants Mormons to be unquestioning—something I believe goes against church teachings and portrays great insecurity. I worked in public affairs for the church for thirteen years, and I had to lie all the time, and this has really battered my faith."[33]

According to an October 10, 1993 article that appeared in the *Arizona Republic*, Pulitzer Prize-winning cartoonist Steve Benson, first grandson of now-deceased Mormon Church president Ezra Taft Benson, resigned from the church. His wife, Mary Ann, also resigned, "to protest what they believe is an increasingly intolerant church leadership."

The church's attempt to silence anyone who dares step outside the boundary of strict Mormon theology only proves that its leaders are more concerned with public image—maintaining the Osmond Family Syndrome—than they are with truth. This makes it very difficult for those Mormon "dissidents" who must live and work in Utah Mormon society. They find, as I discovered, that not only are they ostracized from society, but their children and spouses are as well. One woman who was disfellowshipped in the September of 1993 purge, Lynne Whitesides,

---

32   As quoted from the *Salt Lake City Messenger*, "Mormon Inquisition?" Issue No. 85, Nov. 1993.

33   *Arizona Republic* news story, Oct. 10, 1993.

president of the Mormon Women's Forum in Salt Lake City, said in a *Phoenix Gazette* newspaper article that she had been prohibited from speaking about a mother in heaven (Mormon theology holds that God has a wife), nor could she "name the general authorities and disagree with them in public." Although the article stated that Whitesides agreed to use caution in her public statements, she did not agree to keep quiet. "I will continue to speak out on issues that I believe are important," she said. However, she also said that she must consider the impact that her statements have on the lives of her family. "I have to remember my three children who are out in this culture with the same last name."

Having been reared in the United States I thought little about censorship or the implications of First Amendment rights for the freedom of speech and press. I, like many Americans, took those things for granted and felt that censorship would never touch my life. I was to learn, however, that in Utah Mormonism these Constitutional rights are defined within the narrow scope of the church's interpretation; that free agency in the Mormon Church extends only to the boundaries it has set for its members. I had not counted on my freedom to write running headlong into Mormon Church authority. I never dreamed that I would have to defend my First Amendment rights in a church that promoted the doctrine of free agency as essential to life and revered the United States Constitution as a document inspired by God. I was about to get the shock of my life.

13
ଯଠଓଷ

When Reality and Mormon Idealistics Clash

$\mathcal{I}$n the summer of 1978, the illusion about my life as a Mormon began to fall apart, and the path I had followed for the previous eight years started taking some drastic turns. That summer Dee and I lost our business. During an investigation, we found out we had an accountant that did not exactly have our best interest at heart. Dee was so busy with the aircraft electronic repairs and taking care of customers, that he hadn't kept an eye on financial things as he probably should have. We trusted too much and got burned. We were both barely thirty and unsophisticated in business matters. It was a tremendous, but devastating and expensive lesson for us.

In fact, Dee was so exhausted from the worry and the months of struggle after we found out how much trouble the business was in, that after it closed he stayed home for several weeks, numb with the pain of failure. Even though the business was gone, however, there were still four children to feed and bills to pay. Somebody had to do something. True to my aggressive, take-charge nature, I decided to get a job. I had worked before and had one skill—I could type. Getting a job to help out during this bleak period in our lives seemed the most logical thing to do. Like most of the Mormons in Kaysville, we lived a comfortable but not extravagant lifestyle, so I was confident that I could earn enough to get us by until Dee was able to find work.

Had we lived in any other community, in any state other than Utah, my getting a job would not have even caused anyone to so much as blink an eye. But in Utah, where the majority of the women—and especially good Mormon women who were obedient to the "advice" of church leaders that they stay home—did not work, my getting a job caused quite a stir.

Everyone in the ward knew within days what had happened to our business, and was sympathetic to our situation. Nevertheless, the fact that I went out one day and came back an employed woman astonished many of my friends and acquaintances in the ward. However, I did not know then just how much turmoil this one act of obtaining a job would cause in my life over the next three years. With all the other battles Dee and I were fighting at the time, including dealing with lawyers and trying to recover from the loss of our business, the last struggle I ever expected that I would have to fight was one with the Mormon Church over my employment status. Nor did I have any idea just how much that action would be the catalyst for so many positive achievements in my life. At that time I did what I felt had to be done. It was purely a matter of financial survival.

Working full time as an inventory control clerk for a major manufacturing company ten miles from home and taking care of the house, garden, and four kids proved to be a challenge, but one I enjoyed. Working in a manufacturing environment was to open up a new area of interest for me that would later be quite beneficial in building my writing career. I met new people, and made new friends, especially non-Mormon and jack-Mormon women whom I found to be warm and open and full of fun, which suited my own personality.

Unlike many of my Mormon friends, who could be fun but were uptight and reserved much of the time, these women seemed genuinely to enjoy life. For the first time since joining the Mormon Church, I began to live a life outside of Kaysville and Mormonism.

Perhaps that is why the church discourages women from working outside the home. There women might discover a life other than the one they had been handed by the church, become independent of their husbands and learn that there is happiness outside the walls of the Mormon Church. Officially, church leaders discourage working outside the home because they believe women are fragile, and the stresses of being in the world might harm their tender spirits. However, an article from the Christian Science Monitor, reprinted in the Arizona Republic on Sunday, July 4, 1982, said that Utah women were entering the work force "faster than women nationwide."

Karen Shepard, a former social services director for Salt Lake City, said, "Women in Utah need to work to make ends meet." Shepard was referring to the large families that predominate in the state. Not only are Mormons obligated to pay ten percent of their incomes to the church, Mormons encourage higher education, which can also be quite expensive, especially if they choose to go to Brigham Young University. In addition, most Mormon boys go on missions which is also a costly venture for many families. Additionally, said Shepard, "wealth is a sign of virtue among Mormons." (This is a perfect example of Mormon theodicy, i.e. the belief God rewards good with good.)

From 1972 to 1982, women in the work force in Utah nearly doubled to fifty-two percent, said the report. That was, ironically, the same period of time Mormon officials were openly fighting the Equal Rights Amendment. That fight reached its peak in 1979 with the excommunication of Sonia Johnson, a vocal supporter of the ERA.

Unfortunately, the report also said that Utah women only earned 54.5 percent of the average male income, compared to 60.5 nationwide, at that time. In addition, sex discrimination suits were almost unheard of, said Shepard. "Women here are more concerned about whether they are being approved of. They are less willing to ask for promotions," she said.

Not only did I enjoy my job, I became quite successful. Over the next three years, would receive several promotions into positions of greater responsibility. Dee eventually found a job, but continued problems with both the state and federal tax authorities over the business meant continuing attorney expenses as we sought legal recourse against the accountant and the tax people. The IRS ultimately began garnishing one-half of Dee's wages, which kept us in a financial bind. Thankfully, my job with its benefits and increasing pay, and promotions kept us above the water line.

One thing did change. We stopped paying a full tithe. In spite of all the stories about how the "windows of heaven" would open to those who continued to pay a full tithe (ten percent of gross income) regardless of the adversities of life, I decided that the church was wealthy enough and could fare quite well without my meager contributions. We needed the money more than the Mormon Church. In fact, no one except the highest church officials knows the extent of the holdings of the Corporation of the Church of Jesus Christ of Latter-day Saints, but some estimates put it at about a ten-billion-dollar-a-year corporation. An article that appeared in the *Arizona Republic* in June,

1991, said that the church collected about $4.3 billion a year from its members plus another $400 million from its many enterprises. Given the rate of growth during this decade, that figure is undoubtedly much higher now.

Failing in one's tithing obligations is a major shortcoming in the Mormon Church, since fulfilling that obligation is at the heart of being allowed full participation in the church. One's payment status does not go unnoticed. Each December during the last two weeks of that month, members are required to go to "tithing settlement," where they declare to the Bishop whether or not they are full, partial or non-tithe payers. If partial or non-tithers, they are given the opportunity to pay up in full at that time, or make payments on the amount due, in order to keep their good standing in the church and be allowed full participation. Thus, tithing is another whip held over members—and their eternal lives—to encourage full payment. Our Bishop explained the church's official stance on the matter of tithing, "The church just wants you to be able to have all the blessings God gives a person who pays a tithe." To which I replied, "Thanks, but no thanks. I've got all the blessings I can stand right now." (Oddly, my bishop never found me to be very funny.)

Although I was not aware of it at the time, the longer I remained employed, the more closely my lifestyle was being scrutinized by the ward members. After all, I was not living the prescribed life of a good Mormon woman. I had left the sanctuary of my home, where I would have been safe, and entered the world. As I neared the end of my first year as a working woman, my friends in the ward began asking me when I would be able to quit work. I put them off by explaining the lawsuit we had against the accountant, and how financially we could not make it on Dee's one-half income. I did not want them to know how much I was really enjoying my job. I had begun to find myself for the first time in my life, and realized how interesting the world really was. I think I knew even then that this one step outside the bounds of proper Mormonism would put my life, as I had known it for the past eight years, in jeopardy.

Those boundaries were pushed even further when, in November of 1979, I had my tubal ligation. I told only two of my closest friends in the ward about the surgery, because I asked them to watch the kids for me the Friday after Thanksgiving, when I was scheduled to go into the outpatient clinic. Again, in any other place besides Kaysville, Utah, such surgery would not be considered a big deal. But in Utah it was a step that could have far-reaching implications on one's standing in the church. Since my last child's birth, in August of 1977, people had been asking me when I was going to have another baby. It was expected that about every two years (or less), a good Mormon woman would be pregnant. It was common for the sisters of the ward to start playfully chiding each other every couple of years about when the next baby would be coming along, but I could only take so much of their teasing. One Sunday morning while waiting for Relief Society to begin, a woman sitting next to me asked when Dee and I were going to be having another baby.

"Oh, I can't have any more children," I replied. "I just had my tubes tied."

Her eyebrows shot up in surprise, but she said nothing. That is until, within a week, half the ward suddenly knew that I had had a tubal ligation and was now sterile. Many of the women in the ward began asking me about the surgery and making a big deal out of it.

Shortly after that, I met with the Bishop, the first of many such meetings over the next year at which he sought to probe into my life. I could not imagine what he wanted with me when he called me to meet with him in his office, but I dutifully went. It was close to tithing settlement time, and I thought he might want to ask me about that. Well, I was right about that much. The first question he asked me was whether Dee and I were paying a full tithe yet. He obviously knew we were not because he had access to the ward clerk's books. I told him honestly that we weren't. He then began the same rhetoric about the importance of keeping up with tithing obligations. He asked me when we were going to start paying a full tithe again, and I replied, "When you start paying our bills out of your pocket."

Then I got the story about the "windows of heaven" and all the blessings we were missing out on by not paying a tithe.

"Well, we've paid a full tithe since I joined the church, and it didn't seem to help much," I said. "We lost our business in spite of the fact that we always paid our tithe and lived by all the laws."

He dropped that subject and asked me when I was planning to quit my job and return to my family where I "belonged." Again, I told him that just as soon as he wanted to pay our bills, I would be more than happy to quit work and stay home with the kids. I did not tell him that I enjoyed my job and would not quit now if we suddenly inherited a million dollars, much less just because he thought I should not be working. But I was not about to let him know that. For all my outward bravado, I was always intimidated by the priesthood authorities who supposedly held my eternal life in their hands. I had come to believe that with a stroke of the pen I could lose my one shot at eternal life in the Celestial Kingdom.

Even though we didn't have a current temple recommend and had no prospects of getting one until we began tithing again, I remained attached to the church. It troubled me, knowing that in the eyes of the church I was unqualified—unworthy—to fully participate in Mormonism. I still participated in the Mormon Church up to my neck. At that time, I did not have the courage nor the wherewithal to extract myself. Therefore, I tried to be polite and even slightly demure and submissive, as it was expected that Mormon women would be, while the Bishop continued to talk to me.

Then he started talking about how the Lord was just testing Dee and me to see if we could be faithful in all things, good times and bad. I sat there listening in disbelief to what he told me. Then came the comment that shocked me and made me the angriest I had ever been at a person in authority. "I hear you've had your tubes tied and that you're talking to the sisters about it, encouraging them to have the surgery," he said.

My mouth nearly dropped into my lap as I stared at him in utter disbelief at what I was hearing. Suddenly I did not feel so polite anymore. "I told two of my best friends when I had it done, and it's no one else's business," I said hotly. "Yes, some-how word has gotten out and some of my friends have asked me about it, so I tell them about it. If they want to have their tubes tied, they're all grown women, so I'm sure they can make that decision on their own."

The bishop was getting very disgusted with me and my attitude. Mormon men are not used to women who talk back to them when reprimanded. "That's not the point, Sister Golds-berry." (I always hated to be called that; it made me sound like a nun.) "Permanently curtailing the birth of children is against Heavenly Father's will. It goes against church teaching and is wrong."

I was stunned. "Well, it might be against your god's will, but my God gave me a brain and expects me to make choices on my own. How many children I want to have is between Dee and me and no one else. I don't need your approval, nor the consensus of the people of this ward!" I stood up to leave.

"I don't think we're through talking," said the Bishop, obviously trying to exert his priesthood authority over me.

"I think we are," I replied curtly as I stomped out of his office. I was shaking. I knew I had committed the ultimate sin by arguing with priesthood authority. But at that point, I did not care.

The following Sunday, I did not go to church. I was too devastated and upset to sit and watch this man preside over the ward. When Dee returned home from church with the kids, he told me that the bishop had pulled him aside for a little chat. "He told me that as the priesthood holder and head of this household, I'm supposed to rein you in and keep you in line," he said with a laugh.

"So, what did you tell him?"

"I told him that you're pretty much your own person, and even if I wanted to tell you what to do, you probably wouldn't do it anyway."

We had a good laugh over that, but I had a gut feeling that this would not be the last we would hear from the bishop. I had gotten his dander up, and no priesthood holder worth his salt would let a woman get away with such a rebellious attitude nor let her have the last word. He had the power to have the final say, and I suspected the worst was yet to come.

I sensed in a most profound way that my Mormon experience was winding down to a close. My life outside the bounds of homemaker and mother and the exciting discoveries I was beginning to make about myself and my potential were distancing me from my Mormon friends and the life of the church. In a few weeks, when winter quarter began at Weber State University in Ogden, I was scheduled to begin taking night classes, something I always wanted to do, but knew would not help my standing in the Mormon Church at all.

Spiritually I was bankrupt, something I had never before felt in my life and something I have never felt since. Going to church on Sundays became a major effort, mainly because of the strained atmosphere that had developed between the whole ward community and me.

I still had several good friends, two in particular who continued to stand by me and love me, but I so strongly felt the disap-
proval of so many people at church that it was horribly
uncomfortable. I learned that ward problems were often discussed in Sunday morning priesthood meetings, and it was clear
after my meeting with the bishop that I was considered a ward
problem. My high visibility in the community, the result of my
involvement in many activities, certainly did not help make me
less of a target. The priesthood men had a duty to protect their
wives from someone who could potentially prove to be a
rabble-rouser. Although no one ever said anything to me, I received the distinct feeling that many of my friends' husbands
told them to distance themselves from me.

I knew that through all this spiritual suffering, I needed to
tend to my spirit. Bible study became an important part of my
life again as I laid aside the Book of Mormon and returned to
pondering the things I had been taught during my youth about
faith and love, things that began to reenter my life like long-lost
childhood friends. I spent hours poring over the Epistles of
Paul, whom I came to view as a friend and one to whom I could
relate in a most intimate manner. If anyone understood the pit-
falls of religious legalism it was Paul. The more I read his letters
the more I began to understand why, after nearly ten years in the
Mormon Church I was suddenly in a spiritually bankrupt condition. I had been living in a society dominated by a religion for
which keeping the law was primary and loving the individual
was secondary—entirely opposite of what I had been taught in
my Christian upbringing. I began to tread the long road toward
regaining my spirit, which I had lost somewhere in the wilderness of Mormonism. I was now truly a stranger in Zion.

14

৪০০৪

Spiritual Bankruptcy

$\mathcal{I}$t isn't easy to find churches other than those of the Mormon persuasion in Utah, particularly in small towns. There was, however, one congregation of about fifty people that began meeting in Kaysville. They had managed to buy some property and construct a tiny chapel with classrooms in the basement. It even had a steeple with a cross on top, which was a welcome sight to me as I pulled into the parking lot on a cold, snowy Sunday evening in January. Their pastor was a young man with a lot of enthusiasm, which was a necessity for him to survive as a small minnow in the sea of Utah Mormonism.

I slipped into the evening worship service and sat toward the back of the chapel, joining in as they sang the familiar hymns of my childhood. I began to feel at peace there almost immediately—a peace that I had not felt in many years. Protestant Christians living in Utah, especially in a small-town atmosphere, develop a strong camaraderie mainly because they are so terribly outnumbered. The people at the little church never asked questions and did not really care why I was there—a stranger in their midst—or whether I would join their church. They were friendly and kind, just accepting the fact that I was there among them out of the same need that they were, and shared their love with me on that basis alone. I knew I had come home.

However, I continued to maintain my ties to my Mormon ward, seeing to it that our children went to Sunday school and youth groups every week. Dee did not mind where I went to church, as the attitude of most of the people in the ward was starting to turn him off also. He had been a jack-Mormon when I met him, and with the problems we were having dealing with the church, he had become even more indifferent to Mormonism than when I had first known him.

One evening as we sat discussing the turn our lives had taken over the past two years, and wondering about the outcome of the lawsuit—would we win, or lose everything we owned—Dee remarked about how strange it was that when we first came to Kaysville and were living lives exactly like every other "good" Mormon in town, that everyone loved us. Now that our lives had detoured and we had been forced to adjust our lifestyle to meet those new challenges, we were being abandoned by those same people. It was a heavy lesson for both of us, one neither of us has ever forgotten.

Always an emotionally distant person, Dee had become increasingly more so since the turmoil began in our lives. When he wasn't working, he buried himself in science fiction books, his favorite genre, scarcely aware of the kids or me or the world that swirled tumultuously around him. The sadness that had marked him, which resulted from a traumatic childhood, now seemed to engulf him. He appeared perpetually sad, as if life was carrying him off into an unknown abyss he was powerless to avoid. I did not know what to do for him. After all, there were four children to think of and care for; I had my hands full.

For me, the experience began to lift me back into my faith, a faith with which I had grown up. For Dee, it was the end of his faith in anything connected with organized religion or God. It is a shame that Mormons are raised to have such all-consuming faith in the church and in its leaders, the organization, and its history. Once that faith is destroyed, many ex-Mormons desert religion—and God—entirely. It is difficult for them to believe that God exists outside the realm of Mormonism. In a talk given by Harold B. Lee at the October, 1950, General Conference of the church, he said, "Unless every member of this church gains for himself an unshakable testimony of the divinity of this church, he will be among those who will be deceived in this day when [Mormons] are going to be tried and tested. Only those will survive who have gained for themselves that testimony."

Hardly is there a mention of faith in God within the Mormon Church, or a personal relationship with Jesus Christ, or accepting as one's personal savior. Sonia Johnson said in her book that Mormons are taught "to rely more upon their spiritual leaders for spiritual direction and less upon our own personal relationship with deity." She went on to say that she believes it "stems from a desire in the hearts of the leaders to gain ever more control over our lives." I came to believe that. Although Dee is no longer an active Mormon, the church still holds him in its powerful, far-reaching grasp.

It is crucial for converts such as myself to have a testimony of Joseph Smith, for belief in him is more important to the salvation of Mormons than is belief in Jesus Christ. In fact, although Mormons proclaim to the world that they are Christians, they do not believe that faith in Christ is enough; faith in Joseph Smith as a prophet of God is the real essence of salvation in Mormonism. Joseph Fielding Smith in *Doctrines of Salvation* said, "There is no salvation without accepting Joseph Smith . . . No man can reject that testimony [i.e. that Joseph Smith is a prophet and restored the true church of God on earth] without incurring the most dreadful consequences, for he cannot enter the kingdom of God." Brigham Young declared in his *Journal of Discourses*, ". . . Joseph Smith (is the) passport to [Mormons] entrance into the mansion above where God and Christ are . . ." Mormons are taught to have unquestioning faith in their leaders. In a speech given on February 26, 1980, Ezra Taft Benson, the president and prophet of the church until his death in 1994, said, "Keep your eye on the President of the Church. If he ever tells you to do anything and it is wrong, and you do it, the Lord will bless you for it."

Church members are continually warned by their leaders not to criticize the leaders of the church or its doctrines, at the peril of losing their eternal life. In October 1985, during a General Conference of the church, Elder James E. Faust of the church's Council of the Twelve Apostles, said that church members who criticize their religious leaders or church teachings place their souls in danger. "I cannot help but wonder if a member of the church does not place himself in some spiritual peril when publicly disparaging the prophetic calling of Joseph Smith, or his successors, or any of the fundamental, settled doctrines of the church," he said. This address came at a time when controversy was swirling around recently uncovered letters that showed Joseph Smith to be a dabbler in the occult, which started many of the faithful questioning the veracity of Smith's original testimony concerning finding and translating the golden plates into what became known as the Book of Mormon.

Listening to the conferences of the church on television each October and April, I could almost feel myself being lulled into a form of hypnosis by the slow, sing-songy way of speaking that each of the General Authorities used, as if they all took lessons from the same speech teacher. The unnaturalness of the tone, seemed as if were meant to subliminally lull us into some kind of religious numbness. Later, I realized that the tone was a condescending one to make us feel like little children being spoken to by our authority figures, hence the term "general authorities." Their constant admonitions not to question this authority was an overriding theme each six months.

My questioning of Mormonism began long before that discovery, and I knew that sooner or later my doubts about Mormonism's theology would cause me to fall out of favor with the church. About the same time that I started questioning the church's doctrine and the infallibility of its leaders, Jim Jones led more than nine hundred of his followers to their deaths by ordering them to drink cyanide-laced Kool-Aid™ in their commune in the jungles of Guyana. I remember thinking about that horrible 1978 tragedy and how the leaders of Mormonism were increasing their pressure on adherents to strengthen the church's position among its members by demanding total, unquestioning obedience and loyalty. In my mind, I envisioned all of us lined up on Temple Square in downtown Salt Lake City, with our Kool-Aid™ cups in hand, waiting to do the bidding—unquestioning—of Mormon Church leaders. The Mormon Church does not tolerate independent thinking. "When our leaders speak, the thinking has been done," stated one General Authority. In 1978, the Young Women General President Elaine Cannon put it like this, "When the prophet speaks, sisters, the debate is over . . ."

Some might think that such comparisons are too far out; that a horrible tragedy like the one in Guyana could never happen in the United States of America among a group of people that appears to be so mainstream Americana. I submit that it is always dangerous when a group of people puts its faith and trust in one individual. Any group that demands unquestioned loyalty to its leaders and punishes those who dare ask questions or think for themselves, is dangerous, I believe, and not to be overlooked.

I feared that someone would find out that I was attending another church and that I was undergoing a religious and spiritual metamorphosis that would take me further from the fold of Mormonism. Since the Mormon Church believed that all other churches taught a "perverted" gospel, if it were known that I was attending a different church, I would find myself in the same position as my friend Beth, who was continually in hot water over her attachment to her Protestant friends. And I was not ready for that yet. Other problems were wearing me down.

The loss of the business and the changes that brought about in our life were taking their toll on our marriage. In addition, our oldest son was diagnosed with obsessive-compulsive disorder. Always an exceptionally neat child whose personal rule was a "place for everything and everything in its place," his penchant for neatness had turned into an obsession. Because he was a straight "A" student and an Eagle Scout by age fourteen, I had tried to ignore his increasingly strange behavior. He washed his hands continually and refused to touch anything that anyone else touched. At school, he would wait until someone else opened the door and then slip in behind them to avoid touching doorknobs. He opened the refrigerator door from the bottom with his foot and always washed his plate and silverware before eating. His condition kept getting worse.

I knew he needed to see a psychologist, so I found one at the Davis County Mental Health Clinic. Fortunately for me, the man was NOT a Mormon. It only took him one session to diagnose my son as having OCD. Dr. Bob Fredrickson also had a private practice in Bountiful. Because of my concern that the Mormons who worked at the clinic would become aware of our problem, Dr. Fredrickson suggested that we come to his private practice. I already knew of the dangers that living in the fishbowl of a Mormon town like Kaysville presented. There are no secrets among the priesthood. A few years earlier, a terrible tragedy had taken the life of a woman who had gone to the mental health center for help.

This good Mormon woman, a wife and mother of six children, had gone to the clinic for help. Her husband had moved out of their bedroom to the basement after the birth of their last child, because he did not want more children. Since he did not believe in birth control, absolute celibacy was his only solution. His wife, understandably, became terribly lonely and sought to find comfort by confiding in a man with whom she worked. (The dangers for women of being outside the sanctuary of the home rears its ugly head again!) Soon, however, they were having an affair.

She became so distraught that she thought she was going crazy and went to the clinic to find some neutral, objective person with whom to speak. Finding anyone in Utah who was a Mormon and also neutral and objective was rare. Her counselor, who also lived in Kaysville, knew her bishop. He diagnosed that her mental anguish was a result of sin and reported the woman to her bishop. She was under the impression that all of her conversations were protected by doctor/patient privilege and was shocked to learn that her confidence had been betrayed. Her bishop called her in to meet with him and informed her that he knew of her affair and that he had no recourse but to excommunicate her.

There seems to be an unwritten code in Mormonism, "when they're down, kick them." Adultery is one of the few things for which a Mormon can be excommunicated, but much of the decision is left to the discretion of the bishop. At the news that she was about to lose her church membership, which was this Mormon woman's lifeline, she completely broke down. She went home that afternoon and used her husband's handgun to shoot and kill herself. And what was the moral to that story, as it went around town? The wages of sin is death, of course!

I knew of the dangers of confiding in anyone that had close connections to the church. For several months, both my son and I went to see Dr. Fredrickson, whom I trusted implicitly. My son did not, because he thought the doctor, being non-Mormon, did not know what he was talking about. My son finally refused to see Dr. Fredrickson anymore, but I continued to go myself. Things were about to become far worse than I ever thought they could be.

The summer of 1980, Dee became fed up with the IRS taking most of what he made each week. The lawsuit was dragging into its second year, and our marriage was strained to its limits. He had always been a member of the National Guard and enjoyed the military. He missed flying but was bored with flying fixed-wing aircraft anyway, as he had every license he could accumulate. As a result, he entered the Army's helicopter training program. One evening he came home and told me that he had joined the Army Guard and was headed to Ft. Rucker, Alabama, for five months to learn to fly helicopters as a warrant officer. It would mean big money for us, a chance to catch up on bills and to give ourselves a breather. It also meant I would be alone with four kids—one with OCD—a job, school, the garden, housework, and coping with the church. However, I did not raise any objections.

I have always believed that grown people should be able to do what they want to do in life. I had never been the kind of wife that told her husband, "No, you can't do this." Nor had he ever said that to me. I felt that things would be okay. Besides, the money was too good to refuse. So Dee left in August, and I was alone to contend with the kids and the Mormon Church.

15
ಬಂಧ

Crossing the Line

The day that Dee left for Ft. Rucker was the beginning of an odyssey for me that would test the limits of my endurance—emotionally, physically, and spiritually. I knew things would be tough, but what I had not realized was that from the time Dee left I was in the hands of the priesthood brethren of the ward. It was their official duty, I later learned, to keep an eye on me and make sure I did not stray. A Mormon man's priesthood responsibilities include keeping his wife and children on the straight and narrow. If for some reason he is called away from the home for an extended period, then it falls to the brethren to act as watchdogs over his family. The Bishop began calling me into office on a regular basis, questioning me about how things were going at home, and asking if I needed help with anything. No, I told him each time we talked. Everything was fine and I did not need help, but I would call him if I did. If I had been watched before, I now felt as if I were living in a glass house. It was becoming increasingly obvious that my lifestyle was not approved. I was under surveillance by people who had appointed themselves my keepers.

Things within my personal life were changing rapidly. In many ways, I was becoming the person whom I felt very strongly I was meant to be. At the same time, I was trying to maintain some constants in my life by appearing to remain a "good" Mormon. However, I started social drinking again as I had done before joining the Mormon Church. It was not unusual for me to go out after work on Friday with my friends and have one or two drinks.

I have always lived a life based on moderation in all things, something I learned from reading the Apostle Paul's writings. I have never had a problem with alcohol; I can take it or leave it. With Dee gone, however, I had to be home when I was not at work or school. Much of the evening baby-sitting fell on Keith, my oldest, which I realized later was not a good thing for him. I had no options, however, when I had to attend classes at school. I felt I could not ask any of my friends in the ward to baby-sit for me, as they did not approve of my working and going to school. To help me would have been aiding and abetting a lawbreaker of sorts. So, I did the best I could.

Sometimes on Saturday night, I would take the kids to the little Kaysville Theater on Main Street to see a second-run movie. During the movie, while they were quietly drinking their Seven-Up™, I would slip a mini-bottle of Seagram's Seven™ from my purse and discreetly pour it into my Seven-Up™. Perhaps it was my way of straining at the sides of the box, which only a few years before had felt so comfortable. I felt the need to stretch, to go beyond the bounds that Mormonism had set for me. Something inside me told me that I would never be all that I could be within the increasingly tight constraints of Mormonism.

I do not know much about Valium, except what my friends who were addicted to it told me, but I felt then and still do, that if I needed to do any "chemical" relaxing at all, I would rather have one mini-bottle of alcohol in my soft drink than to become addicted to Valium. Besides, Dee and I had let our temple recommends expire, knowing that by not paying a full tithing we could not possibly have them renewed. Whether or not I drank a little alcohol on Saturday evenings was no big deal. I really did not care about going to the temple again anyway. Even during our happiest times within the Mormon community, I had never lost the uneasy feeling that something was terribly wrong with the secretive rites and rituals conducted behind those walls; I had no desire to be a part of that ever again.

My job was going well; I had received another promotion. While Dee was gone, I bought a newer used car—which we needed desperately—in my name alone, hoping that would keep the IRS from attempting to confiscate it. I was taking two classes at school and doing well in both. The kids were all reasonably good. I did not have problems with them, except for Keith's continuing OCD behavior, which caused me many hours of anguish as I struggled to help him. To help me cope, I continued seeing Dr. Fredrickson regularly at his office in Bountiful. My life was far more complicated at that point than I was willing to admit, and I knew subconsciously that without help, I was headed for some kind of breakdown.

Much of the stress I was feeling came from the fact that I'd fallen into that trap of living a double life, the same trap into which I had seen so many of my female friends fall. I wanted desperately to be myself, because deep down I knew that I was a good, Christian person. Being myself was the only way to resolve the feelings I had about my life as a Mormon. I wanted to be who and what those people in my ward in Kaysville thought I was. I wanted to be able to fit the mold, but as much as I wanted that, I also knew that I could never be something I was not meant to be. The Mormon mold was not me. I was not like the people who had basically the same view of life and were knit together in the community by a common thread that ran so deep and so tight that nothing could ever break it.

I had a much different viewpoint. No matter how hard I tried to adopt their lifestyle, I could not be like them. As much as I was like them on the surface, I was a stranger in their midst. Living in Mormonism had nearly become a prison for me and my spirit, one from which I wanted desperately to break free.

I also knew, however, that breaking free in Kaysville would mean the end of my life as I had known it. I had seen others who had either left or just drifted away from the fold; they had become virtual outcasts—alone and lonely in a society where there is only one way, where the church validates life and no other way is accepted. In Utah Mormon society, I learned either you were in or you were out. There was no middle ground. I knew families that actually disowned their own children or other relatives because they were no longer living the strict tenets of the Mormon religion. If they could do that to their own family members, surely I did not have a prayer of being accepted outside the realm of Mormon ways. I continued to attend church at both the Mormon ward and the little Christian church on the other side of Main Street. At the Christian church, I became increasingly convinced that the God I knew and loved, and in whom I had faith, was a God who placed love before law.

Starting my college education introduced the opportunity to begin freelancing articles for the Salt Lake City newspapers, with encouragement on my writing from my English 101 professor. Articles for the *Deseret News* covered subjects such as working mothers and the unique problems they face, humorous pieces (my "Genealogy is a Grave Business" was particularly well-received) and other articles that were not offensive to Mormons. I sold the articles that touched upon the social ills of Utah to the *Salt Lake City Tribune*. Although the same corporation, the Mormon Church, owned both newspapers, the *Deseret News* was considered the church's paper while the *Tribune* was for every-one else. The *Tribune* ran controversial articles and even pieces attacking Mormons and their religion.

That autumn, while Dee was away and the priesthood was watching me, I wrote one of my most controversial pieces ever. It was an editorial essay criticizing Utah's (translated—the Mor-mon Church) openly hostile attitude toward the Planned Par-enthood organization. There was a drive to rid the state of the organization, which essentially had one office in Salt Lake City. Members of the Mormon Church were blaming Utah's high rate of teenage pregnancy on the Planned Parenthood organization. They seemed convinced Planned Parenthood was teaching teenagers how to have sex. The newspapers published articles almost daily on the controversies raging around Planned Par-enthood and its funding. One newspaper article contained an interview with then-Salt Lake City-County health department nursing director, Evelyn Haws, who "characterized Planned Parenthood as insensitive to the local culture."

Unable to stand the irrational rhetoric coming from so many unreasonable people, I wrote a guest editorial for the Sun-day edition of the *Salt Lake Tribune*. The Sunday in December 1980, when it ran was the start of an exciting but also terrifying experience in my life. In part, the editorial read:

"There seems to be three major areas of concern that have been dominating the minds of the citizens of Utah during the past year. They are the high teen-age pregnancy rate, the 'obscene' literature on the shelves of school and public libraries, and the organization Planned Parenthood. For some reason people seem to equate the problem of teen-age pregnancy with 'obscene' (?) literature and Planned Parenthood. They seem almost obsessed with the idea that the latter two "problems" are the cause of the first, and have found an ideal scapegoat. The consensus seems to be that if we rid the state of Planned

Parenthood and the libraries of all literature except Mother Goose Rhymes and Grimms Fairy Tales, the problem of our teen-age girls getting pregnant would be solved.

"In one evening, there were two news reports of purported 'obscene' literature being found in public and school libraries. One, a television story about a Provo (Utah) parent discovering that his daughter had checked out the book *Forever* by Judy Blume, showed the irate parent holding the book and expounding about the inadequacies of a system that would let such material into the hands of teenagers. The second story was a news article about a Box Elder County parent who sent her children into a bookmobile to check out some 'obscene' books. One of the books in question was entitled *You Would if You Loved Me*, and according to the report, 'is targeted at teen-age girls and is an instruction manual in how to say no.'

"May I relate a story of one girl I know personally? She grew up on a farm, raised by fine, Christian parents. The word 'sex' was never mentioned in that home. She began dating at the proper age of sixteen and found that the feelings she was having toward the opposite sex were wonderful, yet terrifying. She couldn't deal with these feelings, yet she couldn't talk to anyone about them, because she was sure that she was the only person in the world who felt like she did. She concluded that there must be something terribly wrong with her.

"There were no Planned Parenthood organizations for her to go to for some practical information. There were no books for her to read, for she lived too far from the library. After nearly two years of fighting emotional battles by herself she decided to give in to her feelings. Being the intelligent farm girl she was, she knew something of the sex life of animals. Using this as her basis for her 'sex education' she figured that the only time a woman could get pregnant was when she was 'in heat.' Needless to say she ended up pregnant within two months after making her decision. That young girl was me sixteen years ago.

"Yes, believe it or not, I got pregnant without reading obscene books. I got pregnant without the help of Planned Parenthood. I did it all by myself, with the help, of course, of my farm-boy, childhood sweetheart who was as well informed on human sexuality as I was. So for those who have fears that teenage pregnancy problems are caused by books that tell 'how to', or by sex education classes sponsored by Planned Parenthood, may I help you lay your fears to rest. No teenager needs a how-to course in sexual intercourse. All they need is the time and the opportunity. The rest comes naturally.

"In my opinion, the parents of this state would be better off to cease their witch-hunting through our libraries and their finger-pointing at Planned Parenthood, and instead use this time and energy to examine themselves, to find ways of dealing with this problem in a constructive and realistic manner. After all, our sexuality is a reality, not a curse, and it's time people stopped treating it as something to be dreaded.

"The answers lie within the walls of our homes. If parents find it impossible to talk to their young people about sex, then our libraries offer many self-help books on the subject of teenage sexuality and how to deal with the problems our young people are faced with. If that recourse is shunned, then maybe we had better consider sex education in the schools as an alternative. It's time we took a long, hard look at our attitudes, at what we've taught, or failed to teach, our youth in order to solve the problems of Utah's high teenage pregnancy rate."

I never really understood just how far some Mormons would go in their reaction to someone who thought differently than they until this editorial hit the paper. Freedom of thought in a society where the predominant religion limits thinking to what is dictated by spiritual leaders who are followed without question, is a dangerous ideal. I began receiving threatening phone calls that evening from anonymous individuals—all of them male—some threatening my life. I took the threats seriously, however I did not report them to the police.

Later I would learn that death threats against those that go against the grain of official church doctrine are common in Utah. In March 1989, University of Utah law professor Edwin Firmage, who was also a member of the church, reported he received more than 150 telephone calls, including some obscene calls and several death threats after he delivered a speech in which he stated that there is no doctrinal basis for the exclusion of women to the church's priesthood. Although at the time I believed I was the only so-called "dissident" who had ever been threatened, I later learned that many dissidents contend with the same things with which I was forced to deal.

I received numerous calls from Mormon women in support of the article—all of them anonymous also—who were happy to see someone finally stand up and say what they believed but could not say because of their standing in the Mormon Church. I knew that my own "standing" in the Mormon Church, which was becoming more tenuous by the day, was also threatened. I received many letters from non-Mormons and Mormons, some signed and some anonymous, in support of what I had to say.

One of those letters said, "How I love you for your most sensitive and intelligent article I found in Sunday's Common Carrier [the guest editorial column in the *Salt Lake Tribune*]. I thank you so very much for your well-expressed views and beautiful truths. Such a breath of fresh air in this hostile climate of sexual repression and uptightness! I endorse everything you said in your article and much, much more."

She went on to tell me of the story of her daughter who, at age sixteen was an unwed mother who chose to give up her baby for adoption. It was not an easy thing for the mother or the daughter. She said that she had been raised Mormon. "I found it interesting and fascinating that my Mormon neighbors would have felt more comfortable had I hidden her in a closet or sent her to live with relatives in another state for a few months. Such hypocrisy in this culture! They give lip service and only that to teaching and discussing sexuality in the home and on the other side of their mouths admitting how difficult or impossible it is for them to do so." She thanked me for writing the article and expressing what she felt needed to be said. This letter was signed.

One of the many anonymous letters that came stated briefly, "I wish to compliment you on your fine article. It took guts to write it, living in this particular area. I agree with you one hundred percent. Thank you for sharing your opinions with all of us." Obviously it was a woman who found it impossible to sign her name for fear of retribution from the priesthood.

One particularly interesting letter came from a Dutch lady, Arendje Aerie V. Wright, living in Salt Lake City. She wrote:

"Thank you indeed, about wonderful [sic], daring, so just, so necessary, article you wrote in *Salt Lake Tribune* and was issued today!

"I do have to congratulate you, for candor and justice!! I also do hope that you will not suffer the consequences, for to tell the truth, one has to suffer so many times.

"Being close to seventy years old, female, born in Holland, I came here 1956 and was amazed that women in 40's, grey hair, big families, not only where [sic] still pregnant, but, so sad, did not know a thing about their own bodies, reproduction; only where [sic] (sorry to say this hard words) breeding machines, following the will or command [of] old man, so called religious leaders.

"I grew up as you, about same, in rural area—I saw animal life. Thanks [sic] goodness, I met later educated, intelligent people, free from denominations. I could plan my children, help inform, educate other women, and real young did volunteer for what was then so active in my country, Planned Parenthood.

"What did they save from pain, agony, misery, unhappiness to us as a couple. Blessings to my youngsters.

"I cut your article out will use it as an excellent example for others.

"Dear lady friend thanks, happiness, peace to you from an old Dutch lady. Aerie."

Another woman from Brigham City, Utah, wrote to say thanks and to tell me that "The Common Carrier article written expressed my feelings completely. Thank you for having the courage to say in print what so many people feel, but never talk about."

As the mother of four teenagers herself, she said that she resented "the lack of information available to them. In our family no question goes unanswered, but because it is such a hushed up subject, I feel too few questions are asked. And, it is easier not to 'rock the boat.'"

One older woman wrote to offer a suggestion that the Mormons use their widely based seminary system to offer an in-depth sex education program, to teach what Utah Mormon parents are afraid to teach.

Another wrote, "Thank you for your . . . article in today's *Tribune*. That took guts, and I'm proud of you! It's really hard to believe that people can be so hysterical and almost completely out of touch with reality as they seem to be about sex education. The propaganda against Planned Parenthood is unbelievable—to me at least."

A fellow writer wrote to say that she had done a personal experience article on teenage sex but under an assumed name. She said, "I wasn't so sure that I wanted to bear the burdens that might come from such public statements. So I applaud your courage. I do hope that you will hear from other people who feel you have done our community a wonderful service, and that those who still want to believe that no one will ever discover sex if they don't read a book will leave you alone! At any rate, I am on your side, and I thank you for doing what you did."

I did not realize just how much courage it would take to endure the threats. Ultimately I decided that I was not willing to lay down my life for Planned Parenthood. One good thing resulted from all the controversy. Planned Parenthood began receiving an outpouring of private donations, according to an article appearing a few months after the controversy began. Evidently all the controversy threw the subject into the limelight, and Planned Parenthood became the surprised beneficiary of those brave enough to voice our outrage at the undeserved criticism of the organization. It was further proof that the majority of people want those services made available.

Even the State's department of health, Family Health Services director said, "We perceive there is a need. We receive an increasing number of people asking for family planning services. Our clinics are full. The county health departments are getting calls requesting services and are asking for money to expand their services." It was something I had long recognized, that in spite of the church's position on birth control, many women—either with or without their husband's knowledge or support—were seeking family planning counseling. I knew that in spite of the threats on my life and the fact that I would probably have to defend my position to the bishop, I was not alone in what I believed. There was some measure of comfort in that.

However, it was at that point that I began to consider leaving Utah. As I had suspected would happen, a few days after the editorial appeared the bishop phoned me again, wanting to speak with me. Even before I arrived at his office, I knew that my article had raised his hackles, and I was about to be taken to task once again for my opinions. I was right.

"I'm going to have to ask you that you quit writing these kinds of articles for the newspaper," he told me with his priesthood authority dripping off every word. "This is against church doctrine," he added, referring to my belief in birth control.

"Did Utah secede from the Union last night?" I asked him ferociously. "Am I wrong, or is the First Amendment to the Constitution still valid in Utah?" This time I was angry from the start and not in any mood to endure a reprimand.

"This doesn't have anything to do with constitutional rights, it has to do with preaching false doctrine," he said, visibly upset.

I replied heatedly: "The Mormon Church teaches that the Constitution is a divinely inspired document, and whether or not I can write to a newspaper and express my opinion has everything to do with my First Amendment rights." I was getting more angry with every word, yet I was still intimidated by the power I knew this man had over me to strip me of my church membership at will. Yet, the fact that this man still had the power to intimidate me made me angry. I was shaking both from the anger and nervousness.

"I'm asking you to stop this or stronger measures will have to be taken, Sister Goldsberry," he concluded tersely.

"Well, I think the church and I have had a parting of the ways. I'll never stop writing." I got up and left his office, wondering just how far this would go. Would I be killed for something so simple as believing in birth control? At that point I really believed—and still do—that Mormons are capable of doing harm to those with whom they disagree. All those blood oaths I had taken in the temple came flooding back to my memory, and I went home in tears, afraid for myself, my children, and for Dee, who had just returned home from Ft. Rucker to find his wife was now infamous among Utah Mormon society.

16

&CB

The Path to the Outside

*I*t was truly the beginning of the end of my Mormon experience. Although I had no idea what the final outcome of my most recent meeting with the bishop would be, I knew I was now being watched more closely than ever. The members of the bishopric, the Home Teachers, and my Relief Society Visiting Teachers monitored my every move. I was seen as a threat to the other sisters in the ward who might be persuaded by my outspoken ways and radical ideas to take up my cause because I had been so popular in the ward. However, they all knew better. They had been members all their lives. They knew that a radical, nonconformist in their midst spelled trouble for everyone. They began keeping their distance. They also began keeping their children from playing with my children. Associations with me could be perceived as sympathy for a troublemaker and would give reason for their own loyalty to the church to be called into question.

The first Sunday in January 1981 was, of course, Fast and Testimony Sunday. I was exhausted mentally, emotionally, and physically. In November, I had come down with a terrible sinus infection that moved into both ears. I had never experienced such excruciating pain and was in bed for nearly a week on heavy doses of strong antibiotics. Only my best friends in Kaysville came to see me and ask if I needed help. My good friends at work came often to look after the kids and me. I was still run down physically from fighting that. Spiritually, I was run down from fighting what I knew by now was a losing battle to maintain my membership in a church I both loved and abhorred at the same time.

Reluctantly, I went to church that Sunday. Dee stayed home with the kids that day. He was exhausted also. Our marriage was not in good shape. He was angry at the church for treating me as it had while he was gone, and he was rapidly losing his faith in an institution he had known since birth as the only true church of God on the Earth. I sat alone in the pew—very alone. By now, word among the men of the priesthood—who had obviously relayed it to their wives—was that I was in trouble up to my eyebrows; their associations with me should be kept to a minimum. As I sat waiting for the church service to begin, I prayed silently for someone to say something that morning that would give me hope, that would restore my faith in the church; that would at least let me feel that God still loved me in spite of all the turmoil I was experiencing. After all, wasn't that what the church was for? To help us through the tough times in our lives, to support us, and to give us hope for the future? "Please, God, speak to me." I prayed in my mind. "Comfort me. Give me peace. Just tell me what to do."

The service started, and I began listening intently for the Holy Spirit—or my inner voice as I called it—to tell me something, to comfort me and reassure me that things were going to be okay. I took the sacrament of communion, as I did every Sunday; as I had done every Sunday since I was a child. Joseph Smith had adopted this ritual from the Disciples of Christ (Christian) Church through Sidney Rigdon, an early convert to Mormonism from the Disciples group. I recalled that the familiar ritual was another thing that had won me over to Mormonism. As do members of the Disciples of Christ Church, Mormons take communion every Sunday.

I settled back to listen for something inspirational from the people who were standing or making their way to the pulpit to bear their testimonies. Sometimes the testimony turned into a travelogue or stories about what happened at a family reunion—something even good Mormons complained about. Testimony time was also when people stood up and thanked God they were not like all those people in all the false religions of the world, a statement that always made my gut twist a bit. It also reminded me of Jesus' admonition to the Pharisees that public boasting is detrimental to the spirit. Fast and Testimony Sunday was never one of my favorite days.

I watched as a good friend made her way to the pulpit. Kathy was never one to stand at her seat and wait for the microphone to be brought, as some people chose to do. She enjoyed being in front of a crowd. She and her husband, Gene, had five daughters, the oldest about fourteen at that time. She began by bearing testimony that she believed the Church of Jesus Christ of Latter-day Saints to be the only true church of God on Earth. So far nothing unusual. Then she began to relate a recent experience.

"Gene and I were trying to decide whether or not to have any more children after our last daughter was born last year," she began. Suddenly, my ears began hurting and I knew it was not from my recent sinus infection. My heart began to pound, and I could feel my face go red hot. I knew what was coming. Inwardly I groaned.

"We went to the bishop to ask him whether or not I should have my tubes tied," she said as she looked directly at me. "He told us that was a decision we'd have to make between ourselves and God and that we should go to the temple to find the answer.

"So we went to the temple, and as we sat in the Celestial room after the ceremony, praying to God about whether or not to have more children, the answer came to us that I should have my tubes tied. So last month, I went in and had my tubes tied, at Heavenly Father's bidding."

I could not believe what I was hearing. My mouth must have been open because suddenly I clamped it shut in anger. White hot tears welled up in my eyes and dripped out the corners. She went on to say how she had even written a letter to President Kimball, then the prophet, seer, and revelator of the church, to explain what she and her husband had decided and to reassure him that they were living all the laws of the church and were good Mormons. She spoke much longer, but my mind was buzzing with disbelief at what I had just heard, so I do not remember what else she said.

What made me even more angry was the fact that I sat there on a Sunday morning, my life falling apart, problems besetting me on all fronts, and all I wanted to hear was that God loved me and cared for me. Instead, I was listening to Kathy justify her tubal ligation before the entire congregation of two hundred people as "Heavenly Father's will." It was definitely a slap in the face to me, personally. She was saying that her tubal ligation was justified because she had gone to the temple and received permission from the Almighty. I had done mine on my own. Therefore, hers was a blessed event, and mine was a sin. Congratulations, Kathy!

When the service ended, I could not get out of church fast enough. I walked through the doors not stopping to talk to anyone, (as if anyone would have spoken to me anyway) and went home in tears. That day I vowed I would never again step inside a Mormon Church as long as I lived. God does answer our requests in mysterious ways. I had asked for direction; in a way, it was granted.

Life was becoming increasingly more difficult. I was having trouble coping with anything except work and school. Dee still did not have a job after returning from Ft. Rucker, although he did have a little income from his monthly stints as a "weekend warrior" for the Army Guard. Stress was beginning to take its toll on me, but in spite of it I kept up my happy front. A lot of things had changed, things that should have made my life—and our marriage—better but it only seemed to get worse.

Despite my personal successes at work, school, and with my freelance writing, Dee was not supportive. He was merely passive about all my decisions. He was more emotionally remote than ever. I did whatever I wanted to do, but he did not really fill in the gaps that were created by doing that. Our oldest son still did much of the baby-sitting in the evenings, while Dee locked himself away in the bedroom reading the latest science fiction book. There were times when I felt I was supporting the whole load, and I came to resent that terribly. Life was not fun anymore. I was not certain that I would survive, but one thing was certain. My life as a Mormon had come to a close.

17

ಬಂಡಾ

The Final Break

True to my word, I never went back to the Mormon ward there in Kaysville again. I continued my attendance at the little church across Main Street. I was knowledgeable enough about the ways of Mormons to know that one did not simply leave the Mormon Church—just walk away from it—and begin attending another church without major repercussions. Unlike Protestantism where a person can decide to leave the Methodist church and go to a Lutheran church without anyone hardly noticing, in Mormon environments everyone notices when you leave. The Mormon Church dogs you wherever you go for the rest of your life. As I explained earlier, your name is never removed from the church rolls.

My oldest son felt the strongest about my changing churches. Deeply entrenched in Mormonism, which he remains to this day, he angrily told me one day, "You're going to hell for this!" That stung my spirit, but I was no longer naive about the Mormons' capacity to tear families apart—either when one joins the church or when one leaves it. I knew it would be no different with me. Not only would it alienate me from my son, but from my parents as well. A few years previously, my parents became interested in Mormonism due in part to my talking about it all the time. After taking the lessons on Mormonism from the local missionaries, they were baptized along with one of my two brothers and his fiancé. I knew there was a good possibility of being left without the support system of my own family if I left Mormonism.

I was in the process of reevaluating my faith and rebuilding my life in the spiritual sense. I struggled with what was right and what was wrong in my life. Although I had spent the last ten years of my life in a religion where right and wrong were as simple to tell apart as black and white, I had learned that there are many grey areas in life. Trying to come to grips with those grey areas involved a long process of learning exactly what being a Christian meant to me. In my processing, I began calling myself a Christian again, something I had not done since being told that Mormons do not call themselves "Christians." I also came to believe that in spite of all that was wrong in my life, I was evolving into the person God wanted me to be, that God loved me, and that somehow I would not be shut out of His love as the church had shut me out of its. Somehow, I learned to accept myself, and all my shortcomings, as I knew God accepted me. I knew that I was not perfect—would never be perfect—but I needed to find my way on my own. The search for truth as it pertains to my life is on going.

I began referring to myself as a Christian openly, not just around people like my friend Beth. That certainly did not set well with my Mormon friends. Coupled with the fact that I no longer attended the ward—although I continued to let the kids go there if they so chose—my new affirmation made me a social outcast. In the eyes of the Mormon Church I was a religious leper, someone to be avoided for fear of contamination. Only three of my friends continued to associate with me, and one of those had a husband who did not like the idea of his wife consorting with a known "apostate." However, she was a true friend, and I was always welcomed in her home. For that, I will always be grateful to her.

The spring of 1981 was beautiful. We had had a lot of snow that winter, and by April the mountains were a brilliant emerald green. Despite my state of mind, I always managed to enjoy the never-ending beauty of the Wasatch Mountains, which had become a symbol of strength to me, as had the Psalmist who said, "I will lift up mine eyes unto the hill, from whence cometh my help."

I had never felt more alone in all my life than I felt at that time, but in spite of that I kept enjoying my successes at work, school, and with my writing. Dee still did not have a job. Nothing in his field was available in Salt Lake City. He was frustrated, I was frustrated, and the kids were feeling that frustration.

One day at work I was walking through the purchasing department on my way back from the copy machine. I had walked through purchasing many times over the past three years, but this time I happened to glance at a bookcase sitting next to a buyer's desk as I turned to say hello to him. Of all the books on the shelves, my eyes fell on the Phoenix, Arizona phone book. Although it was a mere glance, my inner voice said loud and clear, "You need to move to Phoenix." I stopped in my tracks, asked the buyer if I could borrow the Phoenix yellow pages and then took it to my desk. I looked under "Avionics" for a listing of shops in Phoenix. There were several avionics shops listed, and I suddenly got excited. I copied the page and took it home with me that night. I told Dee to get his resume ready, that Phoenix looked like a good prospect for a job for him.

Within two weeks of sending his resumes, Dee had a job managing the aircraft electronics department for a fixed base operator at Phoenix's Sky Harbor International Airport. He took off for Phoenix with just his clothes to start the job, while I was left once again to wrap up things in Kaysville. It was April. I was finishing up spring quarter at Weber State, the kids were finishing their classes, and school would be finished in six weeks for all of us. For once, everything seemed to be heading in the right direction. I contacted a Realtor I knew in town and made arrangements for him to rent our house out until it could be sold. I gave a thirty-day notice of resignation to my employer and prepared to move. Over Memorial Day weekend, I flew to Phoenix to help Dee find us a house. My best friend kept our youngest child—in spite of the fact that she was aiding and abetting a known apostate—while my oldest son, with the help of my neighbor across the street, watched the other two kids.

That was not the best weekend of my life. The terrible strain of all we had been through was showing on our marriage more than ever. Instead of house hunting, we spent time arguing over what direction our lives were taking and how we could resolve the still unresolved issues of the business from such a long distance. Money would still be a problem for awhile, until we could get settled and I could find a job. Our oldest son would still need a psychologist. It was more upheaval added to lives that were already in turmoil. Finally, when I left Phoenix on Sunday, Dee still had the job of finding us a place to live. He had never been a take-charge person, and I had my doubts about his ability to complete this task without my help. At that point, however, I had no choice.

A few days after I'd returned, something happened that would cause me to make a final and complete break with the church. Before then, I had felt neutral toward the whole situation. I am a live and let live person, and as long as I was free to attend the church of my choice, and take care of my life as I saw fit, I felt no animosity toward anyone in the ward, not even the bishop, with whom I had had several "discussions." The kids still went to all the church activities, and I thought things had reached an even keel. Besides, most everyone knew we were moving, so I thought things were smoothing out. I was wrong.

I came home from school one evening to find Keith totally upset and the three younger kids nowhere in sight. A counselor to the bishop, a man I really did not care for because he had an "attitude," had brought church social service workers into the house. They had gone through my cupboards and refrigerator checking to see if there was enough food in the house. Then they had taken the three younger kids and placed them with a friend of mine down the street a few blocks. On top of everything else, the church had declared me to be an unfit mother.

Until that moment in my life I do not think I had ever really been angry. Upon learning what the Bishop had done, however, something in me snapped like a tightly stretched rubber band. Angry does not even come close to describing what I felt at that moment. Rage raced through my whole being, a terrible uncontrollable rage—the kind that causes people to do things they later regret. I telephoned this particular member of the bishopric. When he answered, I let him have it. All the anger and frustrations that had harbored themselves inside me the past few years came gushing out in a torrent of cursing and screaming. "What do you mean coming into my house, going through my cupboards and taking my children, you son-of-a-bitch," I screamed at him through tears. "As if I don't have enough problems, you have to come in and make more."

"We're only trying to help you, Sister Goldsberry," he replied in a condescending manner.

"You're not interested in helping me," I screamed. "If you wanted to help me, then why didn't someone volunteer to watch my children when I was gone to Phoenix? Why don't you come around and offer to do something realistic to help me? You high and mighty men sit on your thrones and love those people who are doing everything according to your standards, and condemn those who are trying to do the best they can under difficult circumstances!"

"We still love you, Sister Goldsberry," he replied, trying to win me over with a pseudo-kindness, his voice dripping with that condescending tone Mormon men love to use with women.

"You only love those who fit your mold," I screamed. "You people don't know the meaning of the word love." I hung up on him, but not before I unleashed upon him a cursing unlike anything I had even known I was capable. To this day, I regret nothing I said to him.

The next morning, my girlfriend brought my children back. She apologized for the church. She knew how hard I was working and all the responsibilities that had been laid on me in recent months. She also knew that all I was receiving from the church was criticism, not help. I told her it did not matter anymore, that in two weeks we would be gone. Nothing the church could do to me at that point could take me any lower. The following Sunday, Keith came home from church and announced that the bishop's counselor, who had taken it upon himself to have me declared an unfit mother, had just been appointed to the position of bishop of our ward. I knew my timing for leaving Kaysville could not have been better.

18

୫ଠୟ

Excommunication

$\mathcal{I}$ jokingly tell my friends when they ask me why I left Utah, that I knew I was in trouble when I saw church leaders heating the tar and plucking the chickens on Temple Square. Although I can laugh about it now—time does dull the pain and anger—it was probably the most traumatic period of my life. While packing to move, I was still in a state of turmoil about all that had happened over the past few years. I had asked to be loved and accepted by a people whose love and acceptance were only available to those who conformed to a way of life in which they believed to be the "right" way. Love and acceptance in Utah Mormon society requires one to be "theologically correct," and I had crossed over that line when I started questioning the church's motives, its theology, and its methodology. My feelings about the church had run the gamut from wonderful to terrible. Life in Utah, for me, had been both the best of times and the worst of times. Moving to Utah had been an exciting, exhilarating experience, and leaving felt devastating.

The moving van left with our furniture. I said good-bye to my good friend who had come to help me pack boxes in preparation for the move. A few other ward members came by to purchase my food storage[34]—fifty-five-gallon cans of wheat, canned goods, and twenty-five-gallon cans of soy-based, protein meat substitute—all the last vestiges of my attempts to be a "good" Mormon. The kids, the cat, and I got into the car and drove to Sandy, Utah, to spend the next three days with good friends, while we waited for the furniture to arrive in Tempe, Arizona.

Three days later, on a beautiful summer Monday morning, we said good-bye to our friends and headed southbound on Interstate 15 for a new life in Arizona. I didn't know what awaited me there, but I knew it had to be better than living in a fishbowl of Mormonism. I felt an overwhelming sense of sadness as I drove along the highway, the beautiful Wasatch Mountains on my left. I could hardly bear the thought of leaving. It was too painful. It was more than turning my back on a religion. I was leaving a way of life—one that Dee and I had worked hard to build together. I had a sense that our life together was over as well. I looked back only once—to watch the beautiful Wasatch Mountains grow more distant as the highway took us beyond the Salt Lake Valley and toward a new life. I was willing to accept the fact that I was supposed to go to Arizona. My inner voice had never steered me wrong. I was doing what I was supposed to do to fulfill my destiny, whatever that might be.

The ten years between my arriving and my leaving had been a religious education that no formal seminary school could hope to offer its students. I often tell people, if you want to know everything religion should not be, join the Mormon Church for

---

34   The church's food storage program is one that encourages members to have two years of food and water stored for their family in case of emergencies. Although having extra staples is always a good idea, the church spends an inordinate amount of time teaching and preaching about how to store food, how much to have, and how to rotate it properly so it does not spoil. There are also many companies, several located in Utah, that specialize in manufacturing dehydrated food products for long-term storage purposes.

a few years. If you want to understand what Christianity is not, become a Mormon for just a while, and you will understand completely the meaning of Christianity. You will also know that you cannot live it within the hallowed walls of Mormonism.

I had learned some of the greatest lessons of my life in Utah Mormonism, the most beneficial being the difference between conditional and unconditional love. As much as I had been loved by the Mormons as a convert to their religion, I discovered that love was based primarily on the fact that I had chosen to be a part of them, to live as they lived, and to believe what they believed down to the last iota. I felt the terrible hurt and pain that "conditional" loving can cause, and I vowed that from then on I would love people as I believe only God loves people—unconditionally.

If I thought that just because I had moved to a different state, the church would forget about me, I was wrong. Within two weeks all of our family records showed up at our new ward in Tempe, Arizona. The church has a tremendous tracking system, and no one is ever lost in that system. Our oldest son, then fifteen, began attending church immediately, while the younger kids, nine, six, and three, and I stayed home until I had time to find a church home in a Protestant church. The elders who were appointed our Home Teachers showed up shortly after we got settled in, and I had the task of telling them they were welcome to visit with Keith, but I was not attending the Mormon Church anymore. This challenged them to win me back into the fold, an idea to which I was not amicable. I still harbored many bitter feelings about the church's intrusion into my life in Kaysville, not to help, but to criticize. I was not the least bit friendly to these gentlemen and made no apologies for it.

Several months after moving to Arizona, Keith came home one Sunday and told me about a young woman—about my age, I guessed—who had been disfellowshipped for "fornication."

The elders were discussing her "problem" that morning in priesthood meeting. I obtained her name and address and decided to call on her one afternoon to see if I could help her. She was living in a small, run-down house not far from us, with five children, the oldest about eleven or twelve and the youngest still in diapers. I introduced myself as a friend and told her that I used to be a member of the church but was no longer active, but I was a Christian, I said.

This introduction must have intrigued her. Katy invited me in. We sat in her small, disarrayed kitchen, and she told me her story, after assuring herself it was safe with me. She broke down and cried as she told me of her marriage in the Mormon temple to a returned missionary and how she believed that her life would be a typical fairy-tale Mormon family life. (The Osmond Family Syndrome strikes again!) She did as a good Mormon wife was supposed to: she stayed home to care for the house and her husband, and she had babies. But all was not well.

She discovered that while she had been occupied with babies, home, and church work, her husband had met a girl at Arizona State University where he was taking night classes; he was having an affair with her. Shortly after Katy's fifth child was born, he announced that he was leaving her and seeking a divorce so he could marry this girl he had met.

Katy was beside herself with anguish, but there was nothing she could do. She went to the bishop of the ward, who gave her food from the church's regional storehouse,[35] helped her with the rent and other bills, and encouraged her to move forward

---

35   Each stake has what is called the bishop's storehouse, which is a huge warehouse that contains all types of canned foods, some fresh local produce—depending on the season—and all kinds of household items. Mormons in good standing can receive help in the form of food and other goods from the bishop's storehouse, but are expected to work in one of the many church businesses to help pay for it. Many work at church canneries, or Deseret Industries, a thrift store much like the Salvation Army or Goodwill.

with her life. After her divorce, she started taking an accounting class at Arizona State so that she could get a job that would pay her enough to be able to afford a baby sitter so that she could work.

At class, she met a wonderful man, in his mid-forties, who took Katy under his wing. She told me he was the most wonderful man she had ever met. He not only dated her by taking her out to nice restaurants and to the movies, but he often took all the children out with them. He bought them groceries when Katy was down to little more on her cupboard shelves than cereal. For six months, he cared for Katy and her children as if they were his own. Consequently, they fell in love. As lovers are prone to do, they began sleeping together. Katy had never been happier, except for one thing: she knew that she was committing a sin.

She began feeling guilty about being so happy in a sinful situation. She went to the bishop for advice and help. His advice was that she cut the relationship off immediately, and the help he gave her was to disfellowship her from the church until she could repent enough to be allowed to participate fully in church activities again.

I could completely empathize and sympathize with her. I felt heartsick for this woman, who had found the love of a good man at a time when she needed love, but was disowned by her church for it. I will never understand what kind of church ostracizes its members at a point in their lives when they need love and acceptance more than anything. The Mormons call this love!

I remember reading a booklet one time based on a speech given by one of the General Authorities entitled, "Church Courts: Courts of Love." It explained in great detail that to be disfellowshipped or excommunicated was actually an act of love. The reasoning was that to allow someone who has sinned to remain in the church would only be detrimental to their salvation. They needed to be thrown out so they could repent and start over again on a clean slate, in order to receive salvation.

I will never understand such reasoning for as long as I live. The Mormon Church is obviously a place for righteous people only. It seems odd that the church believes people who are having problems can benefit from being casted out and told that when they are "good" again, they will be accepted back into the fold. If there is anything that is an antithesis to the basic principles of Christianity, it is this Mormon dogma that people struggling with life's difficulties should be shoved aside until they can become righteous enough to be allowed back in. That people who are hurting, who need love, who need to be lifted up and given hope are rejected by their support system is an anathema to what Jesus taught.

Katy sat at the kitchen table sobbing, confused about her life, in love with a man the church had forbidden her to see ever again. She had agreed because she thought she loved the church more, but now, alone and lonely with five children to rear by herself, she was not sure. She was even more devastated that her "problem" had been discussed in the priesthood meeting. She said the bishop had promised her that nothing would be said to anyone. Of course, the priesthood, which is charged with overseeing everyone's life in the ward, had to know.

I told her the only thing I could tell her: "God loves you, Katy. He loves us in spite of ourselves and because God places no limits on His love, unlike most people do." I spent an hour with her, talking to her about the unconditional love of God and her relationship with Him. As is true with most Mormons, Katy's relationship had been with the church. She did not really understand what a relationship with God entailed. We talked about its meaning. When I left, she was smiling and said she felt better. "I'm glad you came to see me," she said. "I feel so alone.

I think God must have sent you to me." I thought she would be okay.

But she wasn't, and neither was I, as I would soon learn. About a week later, on a Saturday, the doorbell rang. When I answered it, a man introduced himself to me as the bishop of the ward. He had a long envelope in his hand that he handed to me and asked me to read in his presence, so he could answer any questions. I took the envelop and opened it. Inside was a "citation" on church letterhead, telling me I had been "cited" for preaching false doctrine. For this, I was being "summoned" to a church court for a "hearing" at which time I could answer to these "charges." I read the letter, trying to hold back the terrible urge to laugh at the formal "legal" nature of this "citation."

"Do you have any questions?" the bishop asked me.

"Not really. This is a citation, but as long as you don't take any points off my driver's license, I guess it's okay," I said with as straight a face as I could muster.

The bishop obviously did not see the humor in my comment. (Those Mormon bishops never learned to appreciate my humor.) As the authority of the ward, I'm sure he delighted in delivering the pseudo-legal documents. It probably enhanced his feeling of power as a "judge in Israel," as bishops were called, reflecting their duty as bishop.

"How did this come about?" I asked him, curious as to why this particular time was chosen to call me to a church court, when I had not been active in the church for more than a year.

"You visited last week with Sister [Katy] Martin," he said.

"Yes, I did, but so what? Is visiting with a friend against Mormon law?"

"It is when you encourage her to disobey Heavenly Father's laws and make false statements to her."

"And what false statements did I make," I asked, really curious now as to my "crime."

"You told her that God loves her in spite of her sin," he replied, his voice dripping with authority.

"I just told her the truth," I said angrily. "God loves us all, because after all, we've 'all sinned and fallen short of the glory of God,'" I continued, quoting a popular Mormon scripture.

"I'm not going to debate this with you, Sister Goldsberry," he said. "You may show up at your hearing if you so choose, at the appointed date and time. If you have anything to say in your defense, you may say it then."

I closed the door. At last I would have a chance to experience one last "ritual" to complete the cycle of my journey through the Mormon Church: excommunication. It would be an interesting experience I thought, especially since I was not about to let the church have the last word. I knew I did not have to attend the court, but I was not about to pass up the opportunity to see firsthand what transpired at these "hearings." That evening, I sat down and began writing a "thesis," which I would read at my hearing. After all, if Martin Luther could do it, so could Clare Goldsberry.

19
ಐೞ

Church Courts:
Sitting in Judgement

On a hot summer evening in August 1982 I attended my hearing at the church court, a court of "love" designed to allow the church to save me from my sinful self. The "court" was held in the Relief Society room, where a long table was set up with several chairs in a semicircle in front of the table. One of my "judges" met me at a side door and escorted me to the Relief Society room, where six more men were seated behind the table. As I sat down, I was reminded that Dee and I had been married in a Relief Society room very much like this one. It was my first step along the path of Mormonism. How fitting that in this room, I would take my final step off that path.

The man who had escorted me to the room sat beside me in front of the others. I was not sure whether his role was to be my "legal counsel" or just to guard me during this proceeding. The bishop—as "judge in Israel"—presided over the affair, while his counselors and four other men assisted. I am not sure whether there is a significance to the number seven at these hearings, or if that number is prescribed, but there were seven at my hearing.

They sat there, hands folded on the table in front of them, smiling smugly, their faces glowing with sanctimonious self-righteousness. It was a look I had often seen when sitting before priesthood authorities, a look that years before had impressed me as portraying qualities I had interpreted as virtue and goodness. Now I saw it for what it really was, and I was no longer impressed. Nor did I feel intimidated.

My heart was pounding, and my nerves were on edge, but I was already one up on them: the first thing they told me was that they were surprised I had shown up. I told them I had not come to beg for my retention as a member of the Mormon Church or to ask forgiveness, if that was what they were thinking. I had come prepared with a statement, however, and I was armed with my Bible for ammunition. Nothing these men could say to me now could trip me up.

I had studied Mormonism from the outside in and the inside out. Not only did I know the Bible, but I knew all of their scriptures as well, and I knew where their theological weak spots were located. A lot had transpired over eleven years, and if I had not known how to answer the missionaries who gave me the conversion lessons all those years ago, I certainly knew how to answer these men now. I suddenly felt a twinge of intimidation, but the adrenaline was rushing, and I was on the edge—something I knew from my drama days would put me at my peak performance.

The bishop read the charges against me—preaching false doctrine—and asked me if I had anything to say. Did I have anything to say? Oh, I had so much to say.

"You bet I do," I replied firmly as I whipped out my typewritten speech. Those seven men were not going to judge me without hearing from me first.

I began reading: "It is the purpose of organized religion to serve the people, and to provide a vehicle by which people can serve their God. When people begin serving the religion for the sake of the "church" then Christianity has been lost. John Locke in his dissertation "Reasonableness of Christianity as Delivered in the Scripture" says, 'The truth or otherwise of the Christian revelation (truth in the sense of correspondence with fact) is relatively unimportant. The importance of religion lies in its utility as a guide to morals.'

"Christ gave only three commandments: Love God (Mark 12:28-31), Love your neighbor (Matt. 22:37-40), and Preach the Gospel (John 4:18-21)." [The man sitting next to me had his Bible open and was frantically looking up scripture as I read the chapter and verse, I suppose to verify its correctness.] Christ freed mankind from being under the whip of the law because the law was like a thermometer—it showed the people they were sick, but it could not offer a cure. Christ came to offer a cure for what ailed mankind—a prescription of love.

"When religion becomes a whip it is useless. People can be easily controlled by heaping laws upon their heads through the creation of guilt. Guilt is a strong controlling factor for keeping people where you want them. But, Christ knew that this method did not create the kind of person who would be fit for the kingdom of heaven. Thus, through the fulfillment of Christ, law was done away with (Luke 16:16-17, Romans 13:8-10, Galatians 5:14) and replaced by love. Love is for everyone; the law is for those who cannot govern themselves in love (Timothy 1:5-10).

"Christ said, 'If ye love me, keep my commandments.' What commandments were these? Namely, the three listed previously. Search the four gospels. Nowhere will it be found that Jesus gave any 'food' commandments. Indeed, Christ said it was not what went into a man's body that defiled him, but rather that which came out of his heart. (Mark 7:15, Matt. 15:17, Colossians

2:20-22). Yet, you would have people believe they will be denied the kingdom of heaven because they drink coffee, tea, or liquor, or smoke cigarettes. That is blasphemy!

"Where there is law, people will always find a way to circumvent it. I have a good friend who would never risk loss of her temple recommend by drinking coffee—God forbid! So, to get herself going in the morning and keep going all day, she drinks Tab, a soft drink containing probably at least as much caffeine—if not more—than a cup of coffee. Often she consumes six bottles a day, and when she runs out of it, she has 'Tab fits,' even to the point of breaking the Sabbath to buy more if she runs out of the drink on Sunday.

"A few years ago, some Mormons in Utah asked that a commandment be given against all cola drinks containing caffeine. They were told at that time that it was not good to be regulated and governed in every tiny point of law. Yet, a legalistic religion MUST govern in all points of the law or it becomes ineffective due to the fact that people will move to the gray areas to circumvent the law. There is a law against drinking alcoholic beverages. I counseled with a young woman for several months who was on my Visiting Teaching route. She was despondent because she had been married for several months and was unable to get pregnant. The peer pressure to have a baby became overwhelming (another problem in legalistic religion), so she went to a doctor and got a prescription for Valium, to help her relax so she could get pregnant. She began to take more and more until she was spaced out twenty-four hours a day. Yes, there is a law against alcohol, but none against prescription drugs, thus Utah has the highest prescription drug abuse rate of any state per capita, for women between the ages of twenty-five and forty.

"The reason there are no food laws in the New Testament of the Bible is because there is one commandment that would cover all food laws—love yourself and believe your body is the temple of your spirit. If people truly love themselves, they will do nothing to harm themselves (Col. 2:14-16 and 20-22)." [The man sitting next to me was still frantically searching through his Bible trying to keep up with my scripture references.]

"Christ only taught two rituals, and only one of those is necessary for salvation—baptism. The other is partaking of the Lord's supper. There were also three secondary commandments governing things that Christ was concerned enough about to even mention. But they too, had their basis in love for our fellow beings. The first says, 'judge not.' In his great Sermon on the Mount, Christ said, 'Judge not that you be not judged. For with what judgment you judge, you shall be judged; and with what measure you mete, it shall be measured to you again.' And the Apostle Paul said in his letter to the Romans (14:13), 'Let us not therefore judge one another any more; but judge this rather, that no man put a stumbling block or an occasion to fall in his brothers' way.' (This is covered under 'love thy neighbor.') The very act of judging another puts a stumbling block in your brother's way.

"The second 'lesser' commandment was to forgive, which again falls under the 'love thy neighbor' category. In Luke 6:37, Christ included it in the same verse as 'judge not, and you shall not be judged; condemn not, and you shall not be condemned; forgive, and you shall be forgiven.' Forgiving our fellowman is a criterion for our own forgiveness. 'For if you forgive men their trespasses, your Heavenly Father will also forgive you.'

"The third 'lesser' commandment is 'Be ye perfect even as your Father in heaven.' This is a verse that is highly misquoted and misconstrued in Mormon doctrine. Matthew 5 is Christ's Sermon on the Mount. Through this entire sermon, Christ is dealing with the subject of love. Christ lists no food laws, no rituals, no commandments of any kind. He is dealing strictly with mankind's love for his fellow beings. Beginning with verse forty-four, he expounds with 'love your enemies, bless them that curse you, do good to them that hate you, and pray for them which despitefully use you and persecute you; that you may be the children of your Father, which is in heaven; . . .' And in verse forty-eight, he is still speaking about love when he says, 'Be ye therefore perfect.' Perfect in what? Perfect in love, of course. 'Be ye therefore perfect [in love] even as your Father which is in heaven is perfect [in love].' Or as Luke put it in his version in chapter six, verse thirty-six, 'Be ye therefore merciful, as your Father in heaven is merciful.'

"Peter was the Apostle of the law, and he and Paul had several heated arguments over such points in the law such as circumcision versus uncircumcision, dietary laws, etc. It took a vision from God to show Peter that food laws were of no more importance in the Christian life.

"Paul taught that righteousness comes not through obedience to the law but through faith. In Romans 9:30-32, he explains how the Gentiles, with no laws—only faith—attained righteousness; 'but Israel, which followed after a law of righteousness, hath not attained righteousness.' And in Romans 10:3-4 he says, 'For they being ignorant of God's righteousness and going about to establish their own righteousness, have not submitted themselves unto the righteousness of God. For Christ is the end of the law for righteousness to everyone that believes.' And in Romans 13:8-10, Paul tells us, 'Owe no man any thing, but to love one another, for he that loves another has fulfilled the law. For this, Thou shalt not commit adultery, Thou shalt not kill, Thou shalt not steal, Thou shalt not bear false witness, Thou shalt not covet, and if there be any other commandment, it is briefly comprehended in this saying, namely, Thou shalt love thy neighbor as thyself. Love works no ill to his neighbor, therefore love is the fulfilling of the law.' Therefore, the love of God takes precedence over any law that exists in the Mormon Church.

"In closing I would like to quote Paul once more, from First Corinthians 4:3-5, 'But with me it is a very small thing that I should be judged of you or of man's judgement; yea, I judge not mine own self. For I know nothing of myself; yet am I not hereby justified; but he that judges me is the Lord. Therefore judge nothing before the time until the Lord comes, who both will bring to light the hidden things of darkness, and will make manifest the counsels of the hearts; and then shall every man have praise of God.'"

Sitting there in the "hot seat" of judgement, reading to those seven men gave me a strength and courage I never knew I had. They just looked at me, in seeming disbelief. The poor guy sitting next to me was about worn out with the effort to keep up with the scriptures I had been throwing at them. He seemed glad when I quit reading; he closed his Bible with a loud thump.

"Well, Sister Goldsberry," said one of the men sitting to the right of the bishop, "it's obvious that you know your scriptures."

"Of course I do," I replied curtly. "I wouldn't be here if I didn't. You'd still be pulling the wool over my eyes with all your man-made laws, and I would still be blindly following along."

The men looked at one another, some of them trying not to smile, as if they were almost amused by my outspokenness, something they were not used to seeing in Mormon women like their wives. I was then asked to leave the room, while they conferred and took a vote on what to do with me, as if they did not already know. For about ten minutes, I roamed the halls of the church. It was the first time I had stepped foot in a Mormon ward meeting house since that Fast and Testimony Sunday more than a year before. Most ward meeting houses are laid out the same way, so the building felt familiar even though I had never before been there. As I meandered through the halls, waiting for what I knew would be the inevitable excommunication, a sense of sadness overwhelmed me.

Although I knew that I could never be a Mormon—it just went against the grain of everything I believed—my years spent in Mormonism were filled with good times; I had made good friends, in spite of the fact I had also made enemies; and I had learned so much about religion, and the difference between religiosity and spirituality, between legalism and love. It was time to move on. Excommunication would be the final act to cut any ties that might still have bound me to the church.

The door opened, and I was invited back in. The "verdict" was as I had expected: I was excommunicated for preaching false doctrine (one of only three things a person can be excommunicated for, the others being adultery and murder) and being stripped of my church membership, so that I might be given a chance to properly repent.

"We want you to know," said the bishop, "that any time you have any questions about the church you are welcome to call us and ask."

"No, thank you," I replied. "I just spent the last ten years of my life learning everything I always wanted to know about Mormonism but was afraid to ask."

The men snickered at my parody of a recently published popular book. They stood up, while the bishop put out his hand in an offer to shake mine. I gripped his hand and shook it with my own very firm handshake (not in the limp fish manner to which so many women are prone), which must have surprised him, as his eyebrows raised a bit.

"Thanks for the memories," I said, smiling, and walked out the door.

Within a week, I received official documentation that my church membership was no longer valid. I had been officially excommunicated. Nothing survives permanently. Although Dee and I still loved each other, his battles with the IRS and his refusal to attend to things that needed to be done to put our financial lives in order had taken their toll. In October, my divorce from Dee became final also. I had come full circle.

ဆဝ၆

Excommunication does not mean that you are out of the church, just that your status has changed from member in good standing to apostate member. Once a member of the Mormon Church, always a member of the Mormon Church. They continued to keep track of us. The Home Teachers came to see the kids and me, mainly because my oldest son, Keith, was still active. They continued their monthly visits until one evening they began talking to me about my possible return to the fold. The younger man, in a sympathetic and sincere tone of voice, told me that his sister had been excommunicated.

"But, she's working really hard at getting back in," he said, offering me hope in my own situation.

I looked at him with a smile and replied, "You tell your sister that with God, you're always in."

The older man who had accompanied him began to get very nervous as I started explaining the unconditional love of God to this younger man whose sister had been excommunicated. Finally, he interrupted and made excuses for them to leave. They never came back. My son told me that the Home Teachers visited with him at church after that. I guess they could not risk me contaminating the minds of the good Elders with such heresies as God's unconditional love. It might have caused someone to reduce their dependence upon the church for love and acceptance. It might even have caused someone to begin thinking. God forbid! At any rate, that was the last time I ever had Home Teachers or anyone from the church in my house.

Because my oldest son remained active and because my daughter had been baptized as a member, our records continued to follow us through two moves. I had a good job in manufacturing. I purchased a home in Chandler, Arizona, and the kids and I settled in. Dee left his management job with one of the small aircraft sales and service companies at Sky Harbor Airport and moved to California where career opportunities for him were better. My oldest son left to go live with his grandparents—my parents—in Kentucky when he was seventeen. There he finished his last semester of high school. A ward clerk who was in charge of records called shortly after I had moved to Chandler. I was amazed at the church's uncanny ability to track us, but told him that we were going to another church now and did not wish to be contacted again by the Mormon Church. He tried to engage me in a conversation about helping us come back to the fold, but I declined and told him we were no longer interested. That was my final contact.

My only interest in Mormonism continued to be in the psychological and sociological aspects of religious legalism, particularly in Utah Mormon society, but also in the Mormon Church no matter in what state. I expanded my interest in the peculiar aspects of religious legalism to those Protestant fundamentalist groups, which like Mormonism, put rules and judgement over and above love. Since my odyssey through Mormonism, I felt in a much better position than ever to contribute to the understanding of the role of religion in life and society—what religion is and, more importantly, what religion is NOT, and how destructive to the spirit legalistic religion can be. Through Mormonism, I came to a better understanding of what Christianity is supposed to be.

My journey through Utah Mormonism taught me that Christianity is not about being judgmental or critical, wrapped up in all the trappings of religious legalism involving obedience to man-made rules about right and wrong. My trek through the intolerance and conditional love of Utah Mormon society taught me tolerance and unconditional love, and how critical those two things are to our relationships not only with our fellow human beings, but with God. My journey through the exclusivity of Mormonism taught me inclusivity of all people who have the same right to be loved and accepted by God as I do; that no one is excluded by God because of the color of their skin or their sexual preference or what church door he or she chooses to walk through on Sunday (or Saturday) morning. Not only had I come full circle, but I had traveled beyond to find my spiritual place in the world.

The question I am most often asked whenever people find out that I was a Mormon is, "Isn't Mormonism a cult?" Although some of Mormonism's critics contend that it is, I hold that it is not a cult in the strictest sense of the word. Perhaps 150 years ago, when the Mormon Church sought isolation in which to practice some of its more bizarre rituals and behaviors, it could have been called a cult. However, Mormonism has become in the past fifty years, very much mainstream. Mormons are found everywhere, in every country in the world and in every walk of life. They are business leaders, government officials, sports heroes, teachers, bankers, doctors, and on and on. Although doctrinally they still seek exclusivity, they do not seek isolation from the world. Since the changes to the temple ceremony that eliminated the blood oaths, the cultic image has been reduced considerably. Efforts to be perceived by the Christian world as a "Christian" church continue. Recent television ads that offer a free copy of the Bible rather than the Book of Mormon, support these attempts. However, the demand that Mormonism's adherents follow its leaders in blind obedience and the belief that the church is the only church accepted by God continues to be very like cult thinking.

I predicted when I left Utah that there would come a time when the church would be forced to confront itself, be forced to deal with the issues that continue to plague it. The answer can no longer be to excommunicate everyone with whom it does not see eye to eye. It must become an organization that allows for open debate, open questioning, a fearless and open attitude toward its history. Church leaders must recognize that hiding the unsavory portions of church history will not alter that history and will only result in people finding out that their church betrayed them when someone shines the light of truth on the facts it would rather keep hidden. It will also pave the way for other Mark Hoffmanns to commit theological blackmail against the church leaders and put the leaders in the awkward position of having to explain why they withheld the truth from their followers. Nothing the church reveals about itself can hurt it as much as the recent purge of dissidents, showing to the world its intolerance and conditional love toward people, not to mention that the church's behavior smacks of the kind of intellectual suppression found in Communist China and the former Soviet Union.

The women of the Mormon Church must be given the right to be on equal spiritual footing with its men and be allowed options in areas of education, career, marriage, and especially family planning, without suffering through the guilt they are made to feel if they choose an option that is considered against the grain of church teachings. The church must cease its retaliatory methods against women and the men who speak out in behalf of women's positions in the church. Excommunication must cease to be the church's simple solution to some very complex problems, or the church will find itself constantly having to defend itself to an increasingly doubting membership. Despite a missionary force that exceeds forty thousand, the church will find that the headlines it makes will precede them to all corners of the globe. Fewer people will buy into the church's public relations hype by converting. Consequently, the church may find its numbers dwindling, despite efforts to show phenomenal growth each year. Until the Mormon Church leaders come to grips with the social issues and the theological issues that demand an answer—a real solution, not merely purging the membership rolls of those it perceives as troublemakers—it will always have to answer to the rest of society, both Christian and secular, for its dichotomies.

Afterword
৪৩০৪

Life After Mormonism

$\mathcal{M}$y excommunication from the Mormon Church was not an "end" but in many ways only the beginning of yet another spiritual evolution. Yes, there is life after Mormonism. At one time, I considered becoming a "fringe" Mormon, one who although excommunicated still seeks to hold to religion's basic tenets in spite of the church's rejection of the person. I returned to Salt Lake to attend a few Sunstone conferences held each year by and for fringe Mormons—those who have chosen to color outside the lines of Mormonism—and there met many people who like myself struggle with Mormonism's doctrines. The difference between them and me is most of them find it difficult—if not impossible—to break from the church. Unlike many people who are reared in Mormonism from birth, and who, once they are excommunicated, completely leave organized religion, or those who after excommunication, continue to seek affiliation with the Mormon Church albeit on the fringes of participation, I sought to return to my religious roots. After struggling through a few other denominations, including a non-denominational congregation, I found my way back to those roots with the Disciples of Christ Church. I realized finally that I had grown beyond Mormonism. There was a much larger religious world out there, and Mormonism had to be put in the past where it belonged. I had to move on.

Religion continued to be a large part of my life. Even after Mormonism, I clung to the "church," finding my grounding in religion. It served as an anchor during times in my life when I truly needed something on which to hold. At that point in time, I needed the comfort and fellowship provided by being involved in a church congregation. I continued to study religion in America and the impact that it had, not only two hundred years ago, but the impact that it has today on our society. At the large, nondenominational church I attended for a brief period, I took a Hebrew class and began serious study of the Torah.

I remarried, and my new husband and I bought a home in Phoenix. It was just a block north of a small Disciples of Christ Church, so I made the decision to return to the religion of my youth. I had come full circle. Yet, my experiences in Mormonism would forever alter my worldview of religion and its place not only in my life but in the larger society of the United States as well. As I had done since my early teen years, I continued my search for truth—not truth as it would apply for everyone, but that which would be my truth.

For awhile, I was satisfied that what I needed could be found in the Disciples of Christ Church. It seemed odd to me that much of Mormonism's doctrine also had its roots with men who had been cofounders of the Disciples of Christ denomination. Although I had left Mormonism behind, it was still very much a part of my life in a different way.

My goal became to teach others not just about what I had come to believe Christianity is, but what it is not as well.

Christianity is not exclusive. It is inclusive of all people who choose to believe in Jesus Christ. It is not about the law; it is not about sitting in judgement of your neighbor. Christianity is (or should be) about love. It is not about absolute truth; it is about faith and belief, about searching for the truth of God—of all things spiritual—for our lives.

For the next several years, I taught adult and high school education classes on Sunday mornings. Even at this stage of my spiritual development however, I continued to learn, continued listening to my inner voice and letting it guide me along the path—not toward ultimate truth as seen through the eyes of the church—but my own truth. I learned there is a difference. There were lessons to be learned along the way.

In the search for truth, each of us must travel more or less alone. Along the way we encounter others whose search might parallel our own, whose spiritual journeys have led them along similar paths. We might connect for a moment, learn from each other, then move on. But, ultimately, we are each responsible for discovering our own truth, which becomes the reality for our lives.

I came to the conclusion that one man's truth is another man's falsehood. Truth is not the same for every person. If there is any one lesson I have learned through all my journeying through Mormonism and other various Christian denominations, it is this:

Each of us comes from different perspectives in life. Our worldview is reflected in our life's experiences, and often that view changes as we engage in new experiences or as life circumstances force us to confront new realities. As individuals, we have no right to force our truth upon others, to coerce them to make our truth their truth. Ultimately, there is danger in that "missionary" zeal, which can result in the destruction of lives, physically and spiritually.

Searching for truth can bring us into places we might think we would rather not be. It might lead us beyond where we are comfortable into some new realm that presents us with a whole new set of questions for our lives. Searching for truth is always risky because we are opening ourselves up to the unknown, to possibilities that we might have never dreamed existed.

The following story came into my mind one Sunday as I was driving home from visiting a church called the Self-Realization Fellowship, whose members practiced meditation and followed an East Indian religious leader:

Once upon a time, there was a young man who lived in a village far away from any other. The people of this village lived in relative isolation from the rest of the world and believed that in order to preserve their way of life they had to exclude all strangers.

The people stayed close to their village because they had been instructed by their leaders down through the ages that the water in the village well was the only water in the world that was pure and drinkable. All water in other villages was contaminated.

One day the young man decided to go on a long journey to see for himself what lay beyond the border of the village. He was very careful, however, to fill several canteens with water to last him for the time he planned to be gone.

The young man started off and walked for several days without finding anyone. He continued on his journey until he noticed he was running low on water and needed to turn back. But, he lost his bearings and soon found himself wandering in the wilderness. He rationed his water as carefully as he could, but finally one day drank the last precious drop.

"I'm doomed," the young man cried to himself. "There is no more water in my canteens, and that is the only water fit to drink in the world!"

As he lay there bemoaning his fate, another young man happened along. "What is the matter?" the young man inquired.

"I'm lost and can't find my way back to my village, and I've drunk the last of my water," the lost young man replied. "And since it is the only water in the world fit to drink, I'm doomed to death."

The second young man laughed. "No, you're not. Come to my village with me. We have plenty of water in our well there, and it's cold and pure. You can refill your canteens and return home."

The lost young man was doubtful, but he had no choice. He could not just stay in the wilderness and die. So he agreed to follow the young man to his village. When they arrived, he was shown the village well, and he drew up a bucket of water.

It was just as the young man had been told. The water was pure, cold, and tasted wonderful. He drank nearly an entire bucket, then filled his canteens.

"I don't understand," said the first young man to his savior. "All my life I've been taught that the only water that was fit to drink was in our village well, that all other water was contaminated. How is it that your village has such good water?"

"Oh, it's not just our village," replied the rescuer. "There are many villages throughout the world with wells full of good water that will quench your thirst. Good water is wherever you find it."

Truth is truth wherever you find it. Truth does not reside with one religious group or with one person. Often we stumble upon truth in strange and unexpected places, as I did when I attended the Self-Realization Fellowship. I dared step outside the bounds of Christianity and discovered that truth is wherever one looks for it. My journey through Mormonism pushed me to seek for that truth in my life, forced me to go beyond what I was being told was true to find that which would be my truth.

Allowing one person or group to dictate our truth also narrows our view of the world, limiting self-discovery. Often it can result in relinquishing control of our lives to that person or group with disastrous consequences. As life evolves and we become increasingly the product of our experiences, our belief system often changes as well. Anyone who says that the faith they have today is the same they had as a child has failed to mature spiritually. We can no more remain status quo with our spiritual selves than we can with our physical selves. Evolutionary change is a given. Too many Christians shy away from the word evolution. Yet, evolution is very much a part of our becoming what we are meant to be and do.

Often people come to believe that to be acceptable to God we must follow one church, one denomination, or a proscribed dogma—and there our faith journey ends. Spirituality is a journey of discovery. Like any journey it is not where you end up that is important but the journey itself that is crucial to our being.

My journey through Mormonism was just one leg of a life-long discovery of my spiritual self, a part of my evolution of understanding of life that did not end with my return to the Disciples of Christ Church. For the next several years I searched for meaning for my life through the church, even beginning my Masters degree in theology through a program at Arizona State University. My evolution continued in spite of my believing that it had reached a conclusion.

One Sunday morning as I sat in the choir loft overlooking the congregation of a much larger Disciples of Christ church I had begun attending, I asked myself, "Why are all these people here?" That question became one that I pondered each Sunday, as I sat and observed the congregation. "Why are all these people here?"

Then, while pondering this question one Sunday, my inner voice came on and said, "The question is not why all those other people are here. The question is why are YOU here?"

That took me aback. I sat there stunned at this new revelation. Why indeed was I here, I wondered. The more I pondered that question, the more certain I became that I really did not know why I had attended church all those years.

Perhaps it was habit, developed from childhood by parents who faithfully escorted my brothers and me to church every Sunday and for whom religion was a big part of their life. Perhaps it was my own insecurities about life. The church had always been a safety net for me.

Lately however, I had begun to feel estranged from organized religion, as if a chasm was opening up between me and those in the organized church. I did not understand why this gulf was opening now and not years ago after I had left Mormonism.

I began listening more to my inner voice, seeking guidance from that which I could not see but could hear clearly. Then I invited a Native American to speak to my Sunday school class on the Native American religion. I called the nearby Pima Indian Reservation and asked for someone who could speak to our group on this subject and was connected with a man who worked as a social worker on the reservation. He agreed to speak to my class of high school students and requested a meeting the Saturday before to ask questions about my church and evaluate just what he would say. He explained that although many Christians are curious about the Native American religion, many consider it pagan and do not really want to learn about it. I told him we wanted to learn about it.

We sat in a restaurant during the busy Saturday lunch hour, surrounded by the masses. Yet, it was as if we were alone, as he spoke to me quietly and calmly about his religion. My own life at that point was in personal turmoil once again, and his voice was like the calming stream that flowed beside my "Thinking Tree" when I was a child. His words seemed to flow through my soul and touch my spirit in a way I had not been touched in a long time, not even by Christian ministers. I heard nothing but his voice and felt nothing but a sense of peace that seemed to flow from him and pour into me. When I left the restaurant, I knew I had to have the inner peace this man had.

In Sunday school class the next morning, he impressed my high school students with his talk of things spiritual, of living in harmony will all of life, with not seeking to make the world right with your beliefs but with seeking to make your beliefs right with the spiritual world. For me, it was another step in the long journey to find myself spiritually.

It was also the first time I was able to let go of something that I came to realize I no longer needed: organized religion. As I began to grow deeper spiritually, I also came to know that everything I had sought all my life was inside me; that I had always had the answers to my questions, but had searched externally for them. Too often, we become busy searching for the answers outside ourselves and fail to look inward. After all, Jesus told us that the kingdom of God is within.

There have been many times since my leaving Utah and the Mormon Church that I yearned for that perfect time and place when I felt content to be in the "box." For awhile, all my questions were stilled; I had all the answers. But I know now that we never have all the answers, that life is a continual quest, and that the more answers we find, the more questions that arise. That is a part of the quest and an integral part of the journey to becoming all that God wants us to become.

I still return to Utah periodically to see friends or on business. The Wasatch Mountains still pull at my heart when I see their majestic beauty. I stop in Kaysville to say hello to the two best friends I had there—who stayed by me until the end. And I allow myself to remember that part of my life that was both wonderful and heartbreaking at the same time. Yet, even now when I return I feel very much a stranger—a stranger in Zion.

Index